SONG OF LOVE

AN EXPOSITION ON THE SONG OF SOLOMON

by

Gwen Shaw

Published by:
End-Time Handmaidens
Box 447
Jasper, Arkansas 72641
U.S.A.

Cover by James von Doornum Shaw
Lt. Colonel USAF, Retired

ABOUT THE AUTHOR

Gwen Shaw

Ever since Sister Gwen set her feet for the first time in her life on the soil of China in 1947, her heart has belonged to the nations of the world.

It has been her privilege to minister in over fifty countries. She has spent over half her life in Asia and more recently has made many trips behind the Iron Curtain.

The burden of the suffering millions has always been heavy upon her heart and has taken her to places where few women have gone.

Her great love for God and the people of this world qualifies her to share with those who love God's Word these truths which she feels God revealed to her by the Holy Spirit.

At present Sister Gwen divides her time between Germany and the United States where she is the founder and director of the organization known as End-Time Handmaidens Inc.

Sister Gwen has written a book about her experiences behind the Iron Curtain, "Sigi and I." In it she tells about the work they have done in these lands.

Their mailing address is:
End-Time Handmaidens
Box 447
Jasper, Arkansas 72641
U.S.A.

FOREWORD

When the Lord first began to speak to me out of the Song of Songs, I started jotting down on paper the things He gave me. I had not been doing this many days, when, much to my surprise, the Lord showed me that He was going to open the entire book to this generation. The realization of what He wanted me to do in preparing it for the people frightened me. I tried to evade the challenge, but the Lord spoke so clearly that I knew to do so would be disobedience on my part.

Day after day as I sat with my open Bible before me, He taught me Himself. Sometimes the things He showed me made me laugh with Holy joy; other times I wept because of the revelation of His truths.

Humbly, and with no glory to myself, I pass on to you that which He revealed to me.

"AND I WILL GIVE THEE THE TREASURES OF DARKNESS, AND HIDDEN PLACES, THAT THOU MAYEST KNOW THAT I, THE LORD, WHICH CALL THEE BY THY NAME, AM THE GOD OF ISRAEL." Isa. 45:3.

Gwen Shaw

FOREWORD TO FIFTH EDITION

Seventeen years ago when God gave me the revelation of the Song of Solomon and told me to give it to the world, I asked Him what kind of cover He wanted on the book. He showed me the picture of a bride, with long hair and wearing Oriental dress, standing in the early morning sunrise. No artist could draw it. So for three editions, although the cover picture was good, it was not the fulfillment of the vision God had given me. When the publishers prepared the fourth edition, we tried from every source to get the "Lord's cover." It seemed impossible. Even the large professional photo suppliers did not have this type of picture in stock. One tried to compose a picture, but his work was not acceptable. It was NOT the vision.

While the printed pages lay in the printer's warehouse waiting for the right cover picture, my husband and I went to Israel. Early one morning beside the Sea of Galilee, I put on my Indian sari that I had preached in so many times. The sun was just coming up over the Golden Heights as my beloved husband, Jim, took this picture of me. Seven beams of light burst out from the rising sun. One falls across my shoulder.

After seventeen years of waiting, the vision was fulfilled. This is the exact picture I had seen so long ago.

THE SONG OF SOLOMON
CHAPTER ONE

vs. 1. "THE SONG OF SONGS, WHICH IS SOLOMON'S."

Solomon's Songs were one thousand and five. 1 Kings 4:32. But this was the only one worthy of being recorded in sacred scripture. It was his song of songs, for it was anointed by the Holy Spirit. That which is anointed by the Holy Spirit is superior to all other works.

Solomon, with his great wisdom, may or may not have discerned the depth of this song's meaning — The Lord and His bride, which is the church.

Only the soul with his mind stayed on the Lord can have insight into the depths of meaning which lie hidden in this book of treasures.

Often a soul that is crushed by heartache until its only passion in life is a passion for God — will find the key to this book.

vs. 2. "LET HIM KISS ME WITH THE KISSES OF HIS MOUTH; OR THY LOVE IS BETTER THAN WINE."

The song opens with the proclamation of love from the bride. She yearns and desires the love of the Bridegroom and His continual display of affection towards her.

The Love of the Lord, and continual display and revelation of His affections are more to be desired than all else on earth.

More priceless are His love-gifts to us than anything man or angels can receive.

In Christ there is everlasting, undying, unchanging love.

The Love of man may die, may change, may even turn to hatred, but Christ's love is eternally the same.

"WINE" Here the Bridegroom's love is compared to wine.

a. Men drink wine to make them happy. The secret of true happiness is in the comfort of the Lord's love, not in wine, which has only a temporary affect.

b. Wine is a stimulant, a "pick-up", but the quickening we receive from Christ through the Holy Spirit is greater and longer-lasting. *Psa. 71:20* "Thou, which hast showed me great and sore troubles, shall quicken me again, and shalt bring me up again from the depths of the earth." *Col. 2:13* "And you being dead in your sins and the uncircumcision of your flesh, hath He quickened together with Him." *1 Peter 3:18* "For Christ also hath once suffered for sins, the just for the unjust, that He might bring us to God, being put to death in the flesh, but quickened by the Spirit."

c. Wine deadens pain. In our times of pain, whether it be pains of the body or pains of the heart, the Lord has come again and again to deaden the pain.

Many times in the years that I have served God on the different mission fields, I have had the sorrow of parting. I do not know of any pain quite like that inner hurt that one feels when he has to say "Good-bye" to the ones he loves. Often I secretly feared that I may never see my parents again, or my husband, or my children. But God was always so close during those times of heartache. It was almost as if He had stepped into my presence and spoken, "*I* am here." In that moment I felt the warm comfort of His companionship. Immediately my heart was freed from its sorrow. It was so strange; I might almost have thought I had been injected by some kind of medication. I could not even shed a tear. *His* love was there filling the vacancy. No wine or strong drink could work so effectively, or last so long!

d. The indescribable thrills of happiness, joy, warmth and peace of deep, true love, affect one in much the same way as strong wine. If our heart is void of these sensations, then our love for the Lord is dead.

Our relationship of love with our Lord should not be an empty, old, partly-dead love that is void of feeling, but rather a love as strong and pure as the first feelings of true, deep, living love.

In Rev. 3:16 we read, "So then because thou art luke-warm, and neither cold nor hot, I will spue thee out of My mouth." Why does the Lord want us to be either cold or hot? Food that is cold, as a crispy salad, or that is hot, even if only a plate of beans, is full of flavour. But either of these foods, served luke warm, is tasteless. In the same manner we are tasteless to the Lord when we have no feelings for Him. He will spue us from Him.

    e. Prov. 23:32 "At last it biteth like a serpent, and stingeth like an adder." Often love affairs leave a sting of pain through life, but not so with our Lord's love for us.

vs. 3. "BECAUSE OF THE SAVOUR OF THY GOOD OINTMENTS, THY NAME IS AS OINTMENT POURED FORTH, THEREFORE DO THE VIRGINS LOVE THEE."

"THY NAME IS AS OINTMENT POURED FORTH." This term has a double meaning. Look at the word "OINT-MENT." It is both a healing balm and a perfume.

Truly His Name, the precious name of Jesus, is as the fragrance of perfumes to the lover of Jesus. His name, whispered in trouble, soothes the troubled soul. His name, spoken in hope and faith by the sick child of God, brings forth upon the fevered brow the healings of the Balm of Gilead.

In His name is healing power. Acts 3:16. "And His name, through faith in His name hath made this man strong."

To love the name of Jesus is to know the secret of close communion and fellowship with the Lord.

Psa. 69:36. "And they that love His name shall dwell therein."—Where?—the verse before tells us—in Zion, and in the cities of Judah. Zion is the city of our God, the place of His tabernacle. If we know and love His name, we shall have intimate fellowship with Him.

Psa. 91:14. "I will set him on high, because he hath known My name. "We inherit our kingly authority, only if we *know* His name."

"POURED FORTH." Perfume shut up in a bottle has no revealed fragrance. Ointment left in the medicine chest can bring no healing. But they become effectual when poured forth.

a. The poured forth perfume sends its fragrance out to a much larger area than the spot on which it falls.

Our Lord lived His life in one small country and poured it forth on a single, lonely, distant hill, but His fragrance spread through all the earth, until He shall gather a people from *all* nations for His name. Rom. 1:5.

b. Had He never left heaven's glories, we would never have known or loved His name. But when He was poured forth as our sin offering, we realized the fragrance and the meaning of His name, Jesus — "Our Saviour." To become our Saviour He had to be poured forth.

c. The fragrance of His name is lasting; yea, it is even Everlasting.

"THE VIRGINS" — the Saints, the separated, holy ones. Only they love His name, for they alone know its worth. To them it has been as ointment poured forth. Psa. 119:132. "Look thou upon me, and be merciful unto me, as thou usest to do (according to the custom towards those) that love Thy Name."

"THEREFORE" — because His life was poured out for them.

vs. 4. "DRAW ME, WE WILL RUN AFTER THEE: THE KING HATH BROUGHT ME INTO HIS CHAMBERS: WE WILL BE GLAD AND REJOICE IN THEE, WE WILL REMEMBER THY LOVE MORE THAN WINE: THE UPRIGHT LOVE THEE."

"DRAW ME." A personal thing. You must have a deep and personal longing to be drawn.

To draw means to pull. Surely He pulled us out of the miry clay. He alone drew us out of our sin and indifference, but only after our own hearts awakened to our great need of Him, and our souls called out to Him.

Not only in salvation did He draw us, but in every soul-hungry, yearning cry of our Christian experience He has come again and again in tender love to draw us near to Himself.

"WE WILL RUN AFTER THEE." Once you are drawn unto Him, you realize you are not alone in your desire for more of Him. There are others. "We" is this great company of Virgins who love the Lamb and will follow Him withersoever He goeth.

"RUN AFTER THEE." How expressive of the great love and longing in the heart of the loving bride — the church.

So few love Him enough.

As He passes by, He beckons us to follow, and we must hasten to follow on to know our Lord, or we will become distracted by others, by different interests and lose the direction in which He leadeth us.

People walking can gaze about, but when we run it takes effort, and so it is not easy to gaze about idly.

"THE KING HATH BROUGHT ME INTO HIS CHAMBERS." — The most private and secluded part of the royal palace, into which entrance could only be gained by Royal permission.

But when the King sees the wholehearted following after Him, He flings wide the gates and beckons us home.

As virgins we have no desire to be in any other place. The place where He dwelleth is the place we wish to see, the place we long to dwell in with Him.

It not only will be our final resting place, but even in our everyday Christian walk, the heart that panteth after the Lord shall go in and out with Him. In and out of what? His palace gates. We shall sup with Him in glorious royal companionship.

"WE WILL BE GLAD AND REJOICE IN THEE." So many have never found this gladness.

So many know not how to enter into the Spirit of rejoicing because they have never entered into His secret Chambers.

The deep Christian, who knows His King, shall be strong and do exploits because he is empowered with His gladness and joy.

His joy, which He said no one would be able to take from us, His everlasting, eternal joy, would give us buoyancy to swim through waters with currents of adversity, strong and treacherous, which would hinder us from reaching our goal.

"WE WILL REMEMBER THY LOVE MORE THAN WINE." Someone has said, "To love and to lose is better than never to have loved at all."

The life of anyone who has never known deep, magnanimous love is as a picture sketched in black and white before the artist has applied the colours.

The glorious hues of the rainbow have entered into the soul of the person who has known deep and great love.

Love is a thing of beauty, a gift of God.

It is a little of that which was imputed to man when God said, "Let us make man in our image, after our likeness." — For God is Love.

A great love never dies, nor does it shrink, but always shines as a light in a dark night.

Though many years may pass, and times change ones circumstances, a great love is always remembered.

We will remember Thy Love, Lord;

— On a dark night the remembrance of Thy Love will let light shine through.

— On a lonely pathway it will be as though He walketh with us.

— In a time of sorrow every remembrance of His love will comfort us.

— In times of testings the remembrance of His sacrificial love will make a door of escape that we may be able to bear it.

— Yes, even in death's dark valley we will fear no evil. The remembrance of His promise, "I will come and take you to myself", will bear us up on angel-wings.

Always, always, always remember His love.

"THE UPRIGHT LOVE THEE." Yes, these are the true characteristics of those who Love Him.

One group, one likeness of people, "The upright" with one mark that distinguishes them from all others.

A people honourable, in the position that is right. Yes, that is what He calls us. OH! what a title of honour!

"The Upright" can be traced all through the Bible. What are the privileges of this group of Saints?

1. God knoweth their days. Psa. 37:18
2. The upright shall be blessed. Psa. 112:2
3. Unto the upright there ariseth light in the darkness. Psa. 112:2a
4. He is gracious, full of compassion and righteous. 2b
5. The Lord will do good to them. Psa. 125:4
6. They shall dwell in His presence. Psa. 140:13
7. The way of the Lord is strength to the upright. Pro. 10:29
8. They shall be delivered. Pro. 11:6
9. They are His delight. Pro. 11:20
10. Their tabernacle shall flourish. Pro. 14:11
11. Their prayer is His delight. Pro. 15:8
12. Their ways are directed by Him. Prov. 21:29
13. They possess the good thing. Prov. 28:10
14. They are as palm trees. Jer. 10:5

The bride shows no sign of resentment or jealousy over the love which others have for her beloved.

We long that others shall know Him and love Him too.

vs. 5. "I AM BLACK, BUT COMELY, O YE DAUGHTERS OF JERUSALEM, AS THE TENTS OF KEDAR, AS THE CURTAINS OF SOLOMON."

"I AM BLACK, BUT COMELY." In this verse there are two comparisons of the bride which are beautiful word-pictures wherein we see ourselves.

"I am black, but comely" is the first of these.

The R. V. has more correctly translated it "swarthy", or more understandable still, "sunburned."

This is a correct description of a country girl of any land. She lives and works in the open air.

The city girl who now-a-days works and lives without much sunshine longs for "a good tan."

But in Bible days, as in many Eastern lands today, a dark tan was not desired but rather despised as being the mark of a poor class of people.

The Hakka girls of south China wear great, large, round hats with dark curtains hanging from the brim to keep out the sun. These girls work in the fields and are trained to do all the farm work. Later when they are married, they continue in their labours while the husband usually stays in the home with the children. Her lot is a hard one, and often I have felt real pity to see their bodies bent under loads too heavy for them to bear.

The bride was a country girl. She lived and worked in the country and was darkly tanned, but still she knew she was comely.

"Comely" means pleasant to look at, proper, decent.

In current songs of Palestine, town and city girls are called "The White" and country girls, "the Black."

"OH YE DAUGHTERS OF JERUSALEM."

She has now arrived in the King's palace. All about her she sees the city girls with their white complexions. The daughters of Jerusalem look down upon her because she bears the mark of the outcast, the lowly. She reminds them that though she may be black, she is still comely. She goes on to describe herself in another comparison.

"AS THE TENTS OF KEDAR AS THE CURTAINS OF SOLOMON."

Why the tents of Kedar?

Who were the people of Kedar?

Kedar was the second son of Ishmael. Gen. 25:13. His descendents became one of the great Arab tribes that settled in the northwest of the peninsula on the confines of Palestine. Not being sons of Isaac, they were not included in the promises of Israel. Therefore, they were a Gentile people.

The bride of Christ is mostly the Gentile people, who only too well know the despised position that they held with the "daughters of Jerusalem", the chosen ones, the Jews.

The Kedarites dwelt in tents of black goat-skin. We are the "Black-sheep", the marked ones, and yet the Lord, who is the Chief Shepherd, has sought us out and brought us into the fold.

"AS THE CURTAINS OF SOLOMON." The curtains of Solomon were as opposite in beauty to the black tents of Kedar, as the comeliness of the bride in comparison with her blackness.

The curtains of Solomon were made up of beautiful needle-work on the rarest and most beautiful materials of that day, richly embroidered, with needle-work so fine, that at first glance one would think it was the work of an artist's brush.

We have no beauty of our own. In ourselves we are black as the tents of Kedar, but He has given us a comeliness. He has made us pleasant to behold. He has made us decent. His beauty has become our beauty. Through suffering and heartaches we grow into His likeness. "That I may know Him, and the power of His resurrection, and the fellowship of His sufferings, — being made conformable unto His death" Phil. 3:10.

In suffering we become like Him, who suffered for us.

With each painful pin-prick we suffer, a stitch has been added, until at last — that which was black as the tents of Kedar shall be beautiful as the curtains of Solomon.

Let us not despise each heartache, but see it as the Master's preparation of us that we might be worthy to adorn His Ivory Palaces.

vs. 6. "LOOK NOT UPON ME, BECAUSE I AM BLACK, BECAUSE THE SUN HATH LOOKED UPON ME: MY MOTHER'S CHILDREN WERE ANGRY WITH ME; THEY MADE ME THE KEEPER OF THE VINEYARDS; BUT MINE OWN VINEYARD HAVE I NOT KEPT."

In this verse lies the "Cinderella" story of the Bible. She was the despised one of the family, probably because they were jealous of her great beauty. They forced her to do the menial tasks they did not want to do, because they wanted to keep their white complexions.

Yet, their cruelty to her was not unseen by God. He allowed her to go out into the hot sun to labour in the fields, and He saw her there, as He saw Israel when she suffered in the same way under the hand of Pharaoh.

Her deliverance came just at the place where she suffered the most.

One day while out in the fields, she was discovered by the king who brought her into his palace. In his love for her he did not condemn her for her blackness, but brought her into the palace where, he knew that with time and skin preparations, she would gradually lose her blackness.

The King of Kings walked by us one day, as we bent beneath our load of sin and care. He saw in us that which He knew He could use. He saw something in us that we didn't see in ourselves. He called us aside. One look at Him, and our hearts did love Him. One Word, and our hearts did burn within us.

"LOOK NOT UPON ME, BECAUSE I AM BLACK." Don't look at my blackness.

The Christian, washed in the blood of Jesus, whose sins have been washed away and whose life is white as snow, hates to remember the years of sin that made his heart black.

Many would point at the harlot in scorn, the drunkard in disgust, the murderer in contempt, even after these souls have found forgiveness in Jesus' blood.

But the Lord is not so. He sees no more the blackness. He remembers their sins against them no more.

Let us as Christians not despise those who have come through great darkness of sin to join our ranks, as the Daughters of Jerusalem did.

We do not know what they may have suffered before they fell, nor whose vineyards they had to keep, while neglecting their own. While in sin, we were bond-men to Satan. We laboured in his vineyard; we sowed the seed of sin; we reaped what we sowed. Our own vineyard, which the Lord hath given us, we neglected.

vs. 7. "TELL ME, O THOU WHOM MY SOUL LOVEST, WHERE THOU FEEDEST, W H E R E T H O U MAKEST THY FLOCK TO REST AT NOON: FOR WHY SHOULD I BE AS ONE THAT TURNETH ASIDE BY THE FLOCKS OF THY COMPANIONS?"

"TELL ME, O THOU WHOM MY SOUL LOVEST." It seems to me that when love is deep, it is more than just a heart-love, but the very soul of the individual is wrapped up and possessed by a great love.

The Love we bare for Him is a love that fills our whole soul. That is why when we die, our soul goes to be with the Lord. It has been His through our love for Him.

He said, "Thou shalt love the Lord thy God with all thy heart, with all thy soul, and with all thy mind, and with all thy strength:" Mark 12:30.

"WHERE THOU FEEDEST, WHERE THOU MAKEST THY FLOCK TO REST AT NOON:"

Noon, the hottest part of the day, was when the shepherd would steal under the shade of a nearby tree and rest.

Our little shepherdess can find no rest without her Lord.

How strange that one minute she is in the palace and the next we read of her cry in the fields! Yet the bride of Christ does not only live to love Him, but also to serve. We have to return to our menial tasks, which so often, we feel, are a waste of time, when we would rather be in His chambers in communion with Him.

He has said, "Occupy until I come."

I am glad that the work of the bride was that of a shepherdess, for that is what we are too. The Lord has commanded us — "If ye love Me, feed My sheep."

Just over the hill is The Chief Shepherd. He is resting too, with His work all done. Praise God!

"FOR WHY SHOULD I BE AS ONE THAT TURNETH ASIDE BY THE FLOCKS OF THY COMPANIONS."

She was not the only shepherdess. There were others keeping sheep all around her.

In her loneliness she did not seek for companionship in them, but rather in the Lord. "And truly our fellowship is with the Father, and with His Son, Jesus Christ." 1 John 1:3.

Friendship of companions may prove untrue, but the friendship of our Lord is steadfast and sure. He never changes in His affections toward us.

vs. 8. "IF THOU KNOW NOT, O THOU FAIREST AMONG WOMEN, GO THY WAY FORTH BY THE FOOTSTEPS OF THE FLOCK, AND FEED THY KIDS BESIDE THE SHEPHERD'S TENTS."

Now begins the first words spoken by the Beloved King.

When she cries out, "Tell me, O thou whom my soul lovest, where art thou." He immediately answers her.

"And ye shall seek me, and find me, when ye shall search for me with all your heart." Jer. 29:13.

Someone has said, "A seeking soul and a seeking Saviour will always meet." The Lord is seeking for our fellowship.

"O THOU FAIREST AMONG WOMEN." At every wedding, even the most plain looking woman when she is the bride, is the fairest one present. Not another woman there draws the admiration which rightly is given the bride. When she stands in her wedding garments, she has a glow of radiance about her that makes all the other women appear plain.

The Lord loves us. We are His bride. Of all the creatures that live under heaven, that breathe and have life, the bride, His bride, is to Him the fairest of them all. We should thrill to know this.

The wedding garment He gave us, which we already do wear in His sight, marks us out as His bride and gives us a glow of radiance.

"IF THOU KNOW NOT, GO THY WAY FORTH BY THE FOOTSTEPS OF THE FLOCK."

If you would find the Lord, don't stand idle, begin moving. Go thy way forth.

He tells her to look where His sheep are, to mark out their footprints in the fields.

Among the footprints we will find those of the Lamb of God.

Not only has the Lord been pictured as the Shepherd, but also as the sheep who was led to the slaughter, and the lamb dumb before His shearer.   Acts. 8:32.

As we follow in the footsteps of this Lamb, we will be led to Calvary's hill, where His blood was shed as the sacrifice for sin.

The only place to find the Lord is at the cross.   We must follow Him to the cross before we know Him.

If we follow His birth and life, we see Him as the great teacher.

If we follow Him to the cross, we see Him as the great Saviour.

If we follow Him to the grave, we see Him as the great Overcomer, the King of Kings, the Lord of Lords.

We must go forth and follow on to know the Lord.

"AND FEED THY KIDS BESIDE THE SHEPHERD'S TENTS."

We are reminded of the words which the Lord spoke to Peter when He was testing his love.   The words He said were, "Feed my lambs."

The second command He gave Peter was harder to obey, "Tend my sheep."

The third command was, "Feed my sheep."

It is a joy to feed the wee lambs.   One loves the little helpless creatures.

Each duty is harder and leads to one more difficult than the previous one.   As though having found us faithful, He leads us on to another task.

Think of a young mother in her new home. What a joy it is to nurse her first baby as she holds him in her arms!

Later when the child has grown and has developed contrary ways and needs much training and correcting, it is not quite so pleasant and takes much more patience and wisdom to "Tend that sheep."

Finally, the mother stands at the helm of the household, feeding all her sheep, — big, hungry appetites that need to be satisfied. She may have a large family of ten or more children, and she handles her work as capably as she tended that one, first, single, little lamb.

Had she suddenly been given this final responsibility at the beginning of her marriage, she would never have been able to succeed. But gradually God helped her, and she grew into a better mother with her years of work and responsibilities.

So the Lord's first commission to the young follower after Him, the bride who has just found Him and loves Him with all her soul and wishes to abide in His presence, is "FEED THY KIDS BESIDE THE SHEPHERD'S TENTS."

"BESIDES THE SHEPHERD'S TENTS."

He tells us to feed and care for the kids at home.

Our first responsibility begins in the home.

He says that she should stay close to the shepherd's tents. Remember that as the Chief Shepherd, He will be found around His tents. For truly He is the one that John saw walking amongst the seven candlesticks. The tents of the shepherds are His care.

We should not forsake the assembling of our ourselves together, for where two or three are gathered together in His name, there He is in the midst of them.

The Christian who forsakes fellowship with others will not grow.

vs. 9. "I HAVE COMPARED THEE, O MY LOVE, TO A COMPANY OF HORSES IN PHARAOH'S CHARIOTS."

Why does the Lord compare His bride to an Egyptian steed? (steed — American Revised V.)

First of all, a steed is a very spirited horse, often used as a war horse.

The Lord wants us to have spirit. A horse that has no spirit in it, is a lazy horse. He wants us to be a people that know how to fight the warfare of the Saints. A war horse is the bravest animal God has ever made. Read what the Lord himself has said to Job about His horses.

"Hast thou given the horse his might?
Hast thou clothed his neck with the quivering mane?

Hast thou made him to leap as a locust?
The glory of his snorting is terrible.

He paweth in the valley, and rejoiceth in his strength,
He goeth out to meet the armed men.

He mocketh at fear and is not dismayed;
Neither turneth he back from the sword.

The quiver rattleth against him,
The flashing spear and the javelin.

He swalloweth the ground with fierceness and rage;
Neither standeth he still at the voice of the trumpet.

As oft as the trumpet soundeth he saith, Aha!
And he smelleth the battle afar off,

The thunder of the captains,
And the shouting." Job. 39:19-25.

Oh brother and sister, that is the kind of creature He wants us to be, — one who is ever ready, whose feet, as it were, paweth the ground, who standeth not still at the voice of the trumpet, whose soul is ready for the battle.

The enemy of our souls has pointed the sword against us; but Hallelujah, by His power we go forward fearlessly. We will not turn back from the sword. As oft as we hear the sound of the trumpet, we cry, "Aha!"

"Fight the good fight of faith." 1 Tim. 6:12.

"IN PHARAOH'S CHARIOTS."

An Egyptian horse was at that time the most valuable animal alive. Only the king and men of wealth could afford to own one. Even today a valuable horse may be forth £40,000. They were never used for farming in the Bible days.

vs. 10. "THY CHEEKS ARE COMELY WITH ROWS OF JEWELS, THY NECK WITH CHAINS OF GOLD."

There is another translation of this verse which, I believe, is more correct, as the original text is not the same as the one above. Let us study this other translation.

"THY CHEEKS ARE COMELY WITH PLAITS OF HAIR, THY NECK WITH STRINGS OF JEWELS."

The first thing about the bride that made the king conscious of her beauty was her hair. Hair in the scriptures speaks of power. The king was a man of power. But this young maiden had power with the king because of her hair.

That which God seeks for in us, is that we might have power with Him. The church that is without power, is His shame, rather than His glory. Even as hair is a woman's glory, so the power of the church is its glory. The church that is without power is barren. But when she is clothed in power and covered with the anointing, she is beautiful to the King.

"THY NECK WITH STRINGS OF JEWELS."

Where did this poor shepherdess receive these expensive gifts? Surely she could not buy them herself. Then they must have been the gift of the groom.

He has decked us with His love-gifts.

We wear them as a sign to others that we belong to Him.

Precious jewels have special significance.

1. Value. The most precious things we own are the gifts of the Lord to us. He decks His bride with the gifts of the Spirit, which set her apart from the rest of the world. The closer we walk with Him, the more gifts He imparts to us.

2. Beauty. How beautiful is a great sparkling jewel, and yet the beauty of God's gifts surpasses them, as the radiance of the sun surpasses the light of a candle.

3. Durability. Jewels are lasting. Many Chinese keep their fortune in jewels rather than money. But jewels can be lost, whereas our gifts of salvation can not be taken from us. Moreover the gifts and callings of God are without repentance.

vs. 11. "WE WILL MAKE THEE BORDERS OF GOLD WITH STUDS OF SILVER."

"WE" is the king and his servants. Yes, it is He who has given us garments, pure and white with finished edges of pure gold. We have put on the mark of the deity of our God when we wear His garments. Also, in this pronoun we see the Trinity which was included in redemption's plan.

"WITH STUDS OF SILVER."

Studs are fasteners. These are made of silver which speaks of redemption.

He has fastened His deity upon us with the fasteners of redemption. We would never receive of the deity of our God, if He had not redeemed us from our sins. Hallelujah, He has done it all for us.

vs. 12,13.   "WHILE THE KING SITTETH AT HIS TABLE, MY SPIKENARD SENDETH FORTH THE SMELL THEROF." A BUNDLE OF MYRRH IS MY WELLBELOVED UNTO ME; HE SHALL LIE ALL NIGHT BETWIXT MY BREASTS."

Spikenard was perfumed ointment, very costly.   It came from Arabia, India and the Far East.   Wealthy maidens made small bundles which they wore strung around their necks like a locket.

Wherever they went, they carried their fragrance with them.

The bride says that her Beloved was as a bundle of myrrh to her.   Even as the maiden carried her bundle of myrrh near her heart, we who have opened our heart's door to the knocking of the Saviour and have bid Him come in, are carrying Him in our hearts wherever we may go.

As we travel through a world sullied by sin, we need not smell its pollution, for our bundle of myrrh, our Blessed Lord, gives forth a fragrance that overcometh the ugly, the filthy and the repulsive.

He sendeth forth His fragrance from our lives.

vs. 14.   "MY BELOVED IS UNTO ME AS A CLUSTER OF CAMPHIRE IN THE VINEYARDS OF ENGEDI."

This camphire to which the bride compares her Bridegroom is actually a tall shrub known as the Henna shrub.   It may reach 8 or 10 feet tall and has great clusters of lovely white, very fragrant flowers.   When it was in bloom, it was a sight of great beauty.   It is named from a root "to be white."

We are reminded of the great and splendid vision that John saw of our Lord on the Isle of Patmos.   He records that His head and His hair were white like wool, as white as snow.

Again, we remember how He was transfigured before Peter, James and John on the Mount, and His raiment became white and glistening.

A tree has all its glory only when it is in full bloom.   When it is enshrouded with glory, it is a picture of our Glorious Lord, who was glorified with the glory which He had with God since before the world was.

The ladies of the east formerly used the root of this tree to whiten their skin.   When we come in contact with the Lord, the root of Jesse, He whitens our souls.

"IN THE VINEYARDS OF ENGEDI."   Engedi was a place along the west coast of the Dead sea.   It was a small town in a great wilderness.   Solomon had taken advantage of a fountain that was in that district and had planted great gardens of terraced hillsides.

To come upon a beautiful garden as this in a world of wilderness, to stop and rest under the shade of its great hanging vines, to drink from its cool crystal fountain was the joy of many weary travellers.

The Bride says her Beloved was as such to her.   He was her garden in a wilderness, her cool fountain in a thirsty land, her beauty in a place of bleak barrenness.

Hallelujah, truly, our Lord is as a garden to us, where we can come in and rest and be refreshed as we travel through the wilderness of life.

vs. 15,16a.   "BEHOLD THOU ART FAIR, MY LOVE; BE- HOLD, THOU ART FAIR; THOU HAST DOVES EYES."

I would like to link this verse with the following one.

"BEHOLD THOU ART FAIR, MY BELOVED, YEA PLEASANT:"

Three times in these two verses He has repeated this phrase of love, "BEHOLD THOU ART FAIR."   It is as though the Bridegroom is filled with love and wonder towards His fair bride.

To me it seems, as though all of the Trinity joins in the acclamation of praise of the beauty of the Bride of the Lamb.

The bride of Christ is beautiful in her adornment, as we see her pictured in Revelation, — the adornment that she wears for her Husband.   Rev. 21:2.

Truly, she is fair; yes, she is "all glorious within", arrayed in fine linen, clean and white; the fine linen is the righteousness of the saints.

How beautiful she will appear on that day as she is presented to the Lord Jesus Christ!   A wonder to behold, a joy to the heart, a thrill to the soul, her presence will turn all heaven into rejoicing, as the cry will go up, "Let us be glad and rejoice, and give honour to Him for the marriage of the Lamb is come, and His wife hath made herself ready."   Rev. 19:7.

We read, "Blessed are those who have an invitation to that wedding feast", Rev. 19:9.   If they who are among the ones that stand by to watch are blessed, how much more gloriously blessed is the saint whose privilege it shall be to make up the bride of Christ!

vs. 16b, 17.   "ALSO OUR BED IS GREEN.   THE BEAMS OF OUR HOUSE ARE CEDAR, AND OUR RAFTERS OF FIR."

Let us change the word "rafters" to the more correct translation of "galleries."

This is the bride's home, whether it pictures the great house of Solomon or the great outdoors of the forests of Lebanon. Which place it refers to makes very little difference, but we must remember it is the home of the bride.

"Our bed is green".   Many times we have looked down upon a coffin and seen these two words "At Rest."   For the true saint of God, these words are true.   He has found rest, and his bed is green.   There is no death for the saint of God any more than there is death in a healthy green lawn, fresh and fragrant.

Our final resting place is the entrance into our inheritance of eternal life.

"THE BEAMS OF OUR HOUSE ARE CEDAR AND OUR GALLERIES OF FIR."

The cedar and fir trees both are evergreen trees. No tree that God has given man is a more perfect picture of our eternal home in heaven, a home that He prepared for us Himself.

Even as the cedar has an aroma that is offensive to insects, so we remember that we have a treasure in heaven, where neither moth nor rust doth corrupt.

The cedar was known for its beauty, fragrance, and long life. The fir is much the same.

So we see, the picture of the bride's home is one that is eternal, beautiful, safe from any harm, and fragrant with the presence of our Christ. Yes, even the galleries are unshakable and eternal.

"For we know that if our earthly house of this tabernacle were dissolved, we have a building of God, an house not made with hands, eternal in the heavens." 11 Cor. 5:1.

Ten thousand times ten thousand,
In shining raiment bright,
The armies of the ransomed saints
Throng up the steeps of light;
'Tis finished! all is finished,
Their fight with death and sin;
Lift up, lift up, ye golden gates,
And let the victors in.

What rush of hallelujahs
Fills all the earth and sky!
What harping of a thousand harps
Bespeaks the triumph night!
O day, for which creation
And all its tribes were made!
O joy, for all its former woes
A thousandfold repaid!

H. Alford, 1867.

CHAPTER TWO

vs. 1. "I AM THE ROSE OF SHARON, AND THE LILY OF THE VALLEYS."

There are two different interpretations concerning by whom these words were spoken. Many commentators agree that these words were spoken by the bride, which would mean that she is the rose of Sharon and the lily of the valley. I have thought about it a great deal and prayed about it. The Lord reminded me of the many songs that were written under the anointing of the Holy Spirit which have ascribed these words to the Lord Jesus Christ. So let us look at it in this way also and discover why He should be as the Rose of Sharon and the Lily of the Valleys.

Sharon is mentioned in the Bible a number of times. In every instance except this one it has the definite article before it in the original, which would easily translate into "the Sharon." It is believed that "the Sharon" and "Sharon" of the S. of S. are two different places. The first "the Sharon" was a broad, rich tract of land between central and West Palestine. Some scholars believe that the Sharon of the S. of S. was a district east of the Jordan, which is not again mentioned in scripture.

Does it matter very much where the exact location of Sharon is? Can't we just remember that it was a well known place to every Hebrew at the time of the writing of this book? Many Israelites in travelling through the land, which they usually had to do yearly to attend the religious feast days at whatever place the ark was set up, would be well aquainted with these lovely fragrant flowers that grew wildly and freely in every place where they set their feet.

We do not know whether this rose is one of the roses we know, or one of the seven or more species of wild roses which grow in Syria even to this time, or even the narcissus. Any kind of flower is beautiful to the eyes of the traveller.

While travelling in Northwest China, my eyes would always search the hills for the flowers that grew along the way. Always their brightness was a source of cheer.

Jesus wants to be "the rose" that will cheer us as we grow weary with life's journey. He wants us to keep our eyes towards the hillsides, the higher things of life, where we can catch a glimpse of His beauty and receive inspiration to travel onward.

"AND THE LILY OF THE VALLEYS."

Our Lord mentioned the lily of the field when speaking to His disciples. He said that though they did not toil or spin, they were more glorious than all the glory of Solomon. Certainly then, the meaning of these words is deeper than a description of Solomon, who is the one that put them into writing. They are divinely inspired and refer to the Bridegroom, the Son of God. He is all glorious and magnificent in His splendour. He is the Lily of the valleys. I like the plural; life has many valleys, not only one. In every valley He is there.

The lilies grew in abundance, even in the deepest valleys of Palestine, and they grew rapidly. Hos. 14:5. The Lord will abundantly give grace for even the deepest valley-experiences.

And so, whether we are experiencing times of "mountain climbing or walking through vales of tears", let us look for "The Rose", "The Lily; He is ever near to help and to cheer us weary, sinful pilgrims.

vs. 2. "AS THE LILY AMONG THORNS, SO IS MY LOVE AMONG THE DAUGHTERS."

This lily is no doubt the same lily as that mentioned in the last verse. We take on the beauty of the Lord and become like unto Him who loved us. How hard we strive to be like Him, to be clothed in His likeness. He sees us clothed in His robes of righteousness, in His robe of splendour, not because we toiled or spun to make this robe of glorious redemption, but because He gave it to us even as He gave the lily of the fields their robes.

"AMONG THORNS."

He sees us as we grow among the thorns that pierce our sides. He knoweth our frame and remembereth that we are dust. He knows the trials, the temptations that upset us and cause us much pain. He sees the winds of adversity that blow upon us, pushing us against the thorns. He sees us when we flinch with pain.

Thorns are ugly; they are painful; they are despised by the husbandman.

We may be growing among thorns now, but ere long the Husbandman of our souls will come along and remove these thorns from our side. He will allow them to remain only so long. When He sees our spiritual growth is being hindered by the presence of these thorns, He will come suddenly and remove the thorns and thistles that hinder and afflict us.

Even as a lily cannot fight back against the thorns that pierce its side, so we cannot fight back against the many afflictions, but rather bear them patiently, knowing that

> He knows, He loves, He cares
> Nothing this truth can dim
> He gives the best to those
> Who leave the choice with Him.

There is no beauty in thorny weeds. The lily that grows amongst them stands out for her great individual beauty. So when He looks down from on high, He can spot us immediately because we are so different from those around us.

vs. 3. "AS THE APPLE TREE AMONG THE TREES OF THE WOOD, SO IS MY BELOVED AMONG THE SONS. I SAT DOWN UNDER HIS SHADOW WITH GREAT DELIGHT, AND HIS FRUIT WAS SWEET TO MY TASTE."

Just suppose you are walking through the woods one day. All around you are trees: Spruce, elm, oak, maple and pine. Suddenly you smell something different from the green of the forest. A sharp, delicious fragrance makes you realize you are nearing a fruit tree. Suddenly your eyes see the brilliant red of the fruit of the apple tree. You would stop with wonder and gaze upon this one tree. If you had seen it amongst other apple trees, it would not be such a wonder, but here among the trees of the forest, it is rare; it is a wonder.

So is our Lord when compared to all others. Oh, how oft He has filled our hearts with wonder! We have found Him so oft times in places we had not expected to find Him. We wonder at Him, whose name is Wonderful.

"I DELIGHTED AND SAT DOWN UNDER HIS SHADOW."

Of course, that is the tree we would choose to rest under. We would sit close to where the apples are.

"AND HIS FRUIT WAS SWEET TO MY TASTE."

What a lovely surprise to find an apple tree! How pleasant that it was laden with fruit! How surprising that the fruit was ripe and ready to be eaten! It is filled with sweetness. There are no sour, green, tasteless apples on this tree. These apples do not set the teeth of the eater on edge. Each bite is crisp and juicy; you can almost hear the crunch as the teeth take a big, hungry bite out of the bright, shiny, cool, juicy apple.

"Oh taste and see that the Lord is good." Psa. 34:8.

vs. 4. "HE BROUGHT ME TO THE B A N Q U E T I N G HOUSE, AND HIS BANNER OVER ME WAS LOVE."

This banner is actually an ensign made-up of a figure or device of some kind, elevated on a pole.

Every king had his ensign. It might be some emblem, or it might have his name written on it. It was a sign of authority, of royal authority, usually placed on a high hill.

Our King of Kings has an ensign too. It was made of rugged wood and stood on Golgotha's hill. The figure it bore was God's own dear Son. His Name, the Name of Jesus, written by sinful hands in mockery, proclaimed Him to be what God had said He was, in reality, Jesus the King.

For two thousand years that cross has been the Christian's sign of authority. It has never lost its power.

It is the ensign or banner of the Love of God.

No other kingly banner has ever portrayed such love for the people, as this rugged cross on which the Saviour died. — For God so Loved the World — .

Any time we need a Friend we need only to lift our eyes and see His banner, His ensign of infinite and compassionate love.

Always we abide in His banqueting house. As long as we are near the cross, we are in His banqueting house.

Our wayward feet oft choose to by-pass the ground that surrounds the cross of Christ, but when we do, we must sacrifice the love-feasts of His banqueting house, for which our souls do yearn.

vs. 5. "STAY ME WITH FLAGONS, COMFORT ME WITH APPLES: FOR I AM SICK OF LOVE."

Flagons were cakes of pressed raisins. They were considered a great delicacy, often offered to idols. They were a token of affection.

The love-sick bride asks only for these tokens of her Lover's affection. Other foods she does not desire. His apples she had eaten and found good to her taste. This much she desires and no more.

Truly, we are completely satisfied in Him. The raisins, the fruit of the vine, we partake of as a token of His affection towards us, remembering His blood was poured out for our sins.

Oh, that we might so yearn for the Lover of our soul that we would seek only for Him! That we might be as the bride was for her bridegroom! That the love we bear for Him would be a love as strong as that of the love-sick bride!

God, give us love for You like that.

vs. 6. "HIS LEFT HAND IS UNDER MY HEAD, AND HIS RIGHT HAND DOTH EMBRACE ME."

Just think of it! The hands that created the Universe, that put the stars in their place, that formed the sun, the heavens, and all that our eyes have seen and all that they have not seen, are upholding us.

We are held in loving embrace by the hands of our Creator. What then shall we fear? No harm or danger, however great, can touch us when we are protected in His loving embrace.

What more need we of earthly love and human affection, when we remember He lovingly surrounds us with affection.

Are we weary, are we worn and sad? Hear the words of our Lover.

> "Come unto Me and rest
> Lay down, thou weary one, lay down,
> Thy head upon My breast."

vs. 7. "I CHARGE YOU, O YE DAUGHTERS OF JERUSALEM, BY THE ROES, AND BY THE HINDS OF THE FIELD, THAT YE STIR NOT UP, NOR AWAKE MY LOVE, TILL HE PLEASE."

Can't you just see the bride sitting beside her lover and watching over him while he sleeps near her side. She feels she wants to keep him near and safe beside her. She is afraid that someone may come and call him away from her presence.

Oh, let nothing come between our soul and our Saviour. Charge all other attractions and interests to keep away. Even the dearest of families, friends and relatives can come and break the sweet communion we have with our Lord.

Look into your heart and see what one thing seeks to separate you from close and intimate communion with the Lord?

Be awakened to its treachery. Charge it, command it to leave your heart.

It is the responsibility of the bride to guard the intimate communion with her Lord.

Don't look over your shoulder at others who are in the bride of Christ; the finger is pointed at you. You are part of His bride. How is it with you? Have you kept your heart clean of all other affections?

If you have not, then I charge you to awaken and to search your heart, and whatever you find that is not pleasing to Him, charge in the name of Jesus to depart from your life.

"BY THE ROES AND BY THE HINDS."

The roe was some sort of antelope. It was allowed to be eaten as food. Deut. 12:15, 22. It was very fleet of foot. It was praised for its loveliness.

The Hind is the female of the common stag, known for its gentleness, modesty, earnest longing, maternal affection, shyness and timidity.

The cry of the bride rings out, "By all that is lovely, gentle, modest, that I long for and love, I charge you stir not up nor awake my love, till He please."

vs. 8. "THE VOICE OF MY BELOVED! BEHOLD, HE COMETH LEAPING UPON THE MOUNTAINS, SKIPPING UPON THE HILLS."

Hallelujah, Hallelujah, Hallelujah! The cry will soon go out, "Behold the bridegroom cometh — Go ye out to meet Him."

"And the Lord Himself shall descend from heaven with a shout."

Brother and Sister, it won't be long ere our ears shall hear the voice of our Beloved. How oft we have longed to see His face, to hear His voice! On that day we will hear His voice as he cometh leaping upon the mountains, skipping upon the hills. With great joy He will come to gather us home. Leaping and skipping is a picture of great joy.

The voice of my Beloved! No choir sang so grand a song; no voice on earth e're spoke so sweet; no angel of heaven can compare with the beautiful voice of our Beloved. His cry as He comes for us will be heard by every waiting ear.

"Oh how my heart with rapture will praise Him Praise Him for saving a sinner like me."

vs. 9. "MY BELOVED IS LIKE A ROE OR A YOUNG HART: BEHOLD HE STANDETH BEHIND OUR WALL, HE LOOKETH FORTH AT THE WINDOWS, SHEWING HIMSELF THROUGH THE LATTICE."

The hart is the male stag, a member of the deer tribe. It is reckoned among the clean animals.

As we mentioned before, these animals are noted for their swiftness.

"Behold I come quickly" is the warning of the Lord to us. We may at times wonder how much longer we will have to wait. We may feel that He has forgotten His bride. We may even be tempted to say with the scoffers or secretly think in our own hearts, "Where is the promise of His coming?"

Little do we realize that He will come suddenly, as a thief in the night, as a roe or a young hart, suddenly He will have arrived. Silently He will have appeared by our side.

Then, "he that is unjust, let him be unjust still: and he which is filthy, let him be filthy still: and he that is righteous, let him be righteous still: and he that is holy, let him be holy still." Rev. 22:11.

The hunter looking for the deer must have his gun ready at all times; there is no time after he sees the deer to begin cleaning and shining his gun and buying bullets. So it is with us, let us be ready, for we know not the day or the hour of His appearing.

"HE LOOKETH FORTH AT THE WINDOWS."

Surely the Lord is looking forth from the windows of heaven even now. He is longing to come and gather us to Himself.

How wonderful! Oh, how I love to think that He is looking at us through the windows of heaven, watching to see if we are looking His way!

"SHEWING HIMSELF THROUGH THE LATTICE."

"Now we see through a glass, darkly; but then face to face: now I know in part; but then shall I know even as also I am known." 1 Cor. 13:12.

It seems as though at times we can catch a glimpse of the Lord through the lattice. Now and then He manifests Himself to us, and we are thrilled at the realization of His presence and power, but all this is as nothing in comparison to the full revelation of Himself which yet awaits us.

The more we see Him, the more we are changed into His likeness. "But we all, with open face beholding as in a glass the glory of the Lord, are changed into the same image from glory to glory, even as by the Spirit of Lord." 11 Cor. 3:18.

If by seeing Him, as it were, through a glass darkly, or through the lattice wall, we can take on the same image of His glory, how much more shall we be like Him when we shall see Him as He is. When the lattice is removed, we shall see Him face to face.

> Face to face shall I behold Him
> Far beyond the starry sky
> Face to face, in all His glory
> I shall see Him bye and bye.

Even if it means that the angel of death must come and remove the lattice, we fear not, for anything that removes this wall, this barrier, will be a friend to our souls. We would see Christ!

vs. 10. "MY BELOVED SPAKE, AND SAID UNTO ME, RISE UP, MY LOVE, MY FAIR ONE, AND COME AWAY."

How often I have gazed up into the sky and tried to picture the coming of the Lord! I have felt the quickening of His Spirit within me, and it has made me feel that it would be so easy to rise through the sky to meet Him.

Have you ever noticed as you sit in the plane at the end of the runway, as the pilot tests the instruments and increases the speed of each engine separately, testing the magnetos, checking the control movements, it seems as though the plane, vibrant with life, will take off even before the all-clear comes from the control tower.

That describes, in a small way, the readiness, the vibrant life of the Holy Spirit dwelling within us, which quickens our mortal bodies at the thought of the rapture of the saints. But we must wait for the permission from the "control tower" before we coast down the runway and take off into the blue.

Oh, my friend, are you weary with waiting? Has it seemed too long? It won't be long now. Soon the call from the "control tower" will come through, "Rise up, my love, my fair one, and come away."

No one knows what the first words of the Lord will be as He descends through the skies to claim His bride, but it could be that these are the very words He will shout forth for our listening, waiting ear.

vs. 11. "FOR LO, THE WINTER IS PAST, THE RAIN IS OVER AND GONE;"

Winter with its cold, its biting winds, winter with the death and misery it brings to so many, is past. It will be past forever. Our life on earth away from the immediate presence of the Lord, is as winter.

Do you wonder why things are so oft hard to bear? Do you wonder at the pain you must endure? Do you wonder at the testings and trials you go through? This is wintertime.

After the winter comes the cold March winds. April brings the rain; no sunshine peeps through the clouds. You look out of your window and see the clouds in the sky. Life not only has its cold and bitter days, the days of winter; it has its dismal and sad days, the days of the rains.

> God hath not promised skies always blue,
> Flower strewn pathways all our lives thro'
> God hath not promised sun without rain,
> Joy without sorrow, peace without pain.

But on that day, winter will be past, the rains over and gone.

There will be no clouds in heaven. There will be no sorrow there.

"And God shall wipe away all tears from their eyes; and there shall be no more death, neither sorrow, nor crying, neither shall there be any more pain: for the former things (the winter and the rain) are passed away." Rev. 21:4.

vs. 12. "THE FLOWERS APPEAR ON THE EARTH; THE TIME OF THE SINGING OF THE BIRDS IS COME, AND THE VOICE OF THE TURTLE IS HEARD IN OUR LAND."

Glorious springtime! This is the season of resurrection, when the seed that has died comes forth in new life. The flowers begin to appear, sometimes even through the early snows, like the snowdrop of England and Vancouver Island. The birds come back, and with them they bring their song of cheer. The turtle begins its love call. Nests are being built; little, smooth, round eggs are being laid. The chill has left the air; the heat of summer has not yet arrived. Everywhere you feel life.

Our spring time will dawn with the morning of our resurrection.

I am so glad that the Lord arose in springtime. Springtime is a perfect picture of the resurrection of the Lord.

But it also pictures the resurrection of the saints. We will rise, and our bodies shall be changed; this corruptible must put on incorruption, and this mortal must put on immortality. "So when this corruptible shall have put on incorruption, and this mortal shall have put on immortality, then shall be brought to pass the saying that is written, "death is swallowed up in victory." — (The victory of the resurrection). 1 Cor. 15:54.

vs. 13.   "THE FIG TREE PUTTETH FORTH HER GREEN FIGS, AND THE VINES WITH THE TENDER GRAPE GIVE A GOOD SMELL. ARISE, MY LOVE, MY FAIR ONE, AND COME AWAY."

When the disciples asked the Lord, "Tell us, when shall these things be? and what shall be the sign of Thy coming?" He told them that parable about the fig tree.

"Now learn a parable of the fig tree; when her branch is yet tender, and putteth forth leaves, ye know that summer is near: So ye in like manner, when ye shall see these things come to pass, know that it is nigh, even at the doors." "And then shall they see the Son of man coming in the clouds with great power and glory. And then shall He send His angels, and shall gather together His elect from the four winds, from the uttermost part of the earth to the uttermost part of heaven." Mark 13:28, 29, 26, 27.

Some Bible scholars say that the fig tree is a type of Israel, and that her coming together and once again founding the nation of Israel, is a fulfilment of the prophetic parable concerning the fig tree putting forth her leaves.

If this is true, then we know that His coming is nigh, even at our very doors.

"AND THE VINES WITH THE TENDER GRAPE GIVE A GOOD SMELL."

Often, I remember, when driving through the Niagara Penninsula in the early autumn, when the grapes were ripe, how the fragrance of their fruits would waft across the fields and from the sides of the road into our car. We knew the grapes were ripe because we could smell their lovely fragrance.

The vine speaks of the Christian's communion with the Lord, and the grape is the fruit which results from this communion. The fruits of our lives should send forth their fragrance to all who pass by us.

"ARISE, MY LOVE, MY FAIR ONE, AND COME AWAY."

Once again we are reminded of His coming cry which we will hear when "the fig tree putteth forth her green figs, and the vines give a good smell." When all things are ready for His coming, He will appear.

vs. 14. "O MY DOVE, THAT ART IN THE CLEFTS OF THE ROCK, IN THE SECRET PLACES OF THE STAIRS, LET ME SEE THY COUNTENANCE, LET ME HEAR THY VOICE; FOR SWEET IS THY VOICE, AND THY COUNTENANCE IS COMELY."

When God wanted to show His love to Moses and wanted to reward Moses for the obedience and friendship he had always shown to the Lord, God gave him a special surprise. He told him these words as found in Ex. 33:21-23. "Behold, there is a place by me, and thou shalt stand upon a rock: And it shall come to pass, while my glory passeth by, that I will put thee in a cleft of the rock, and will cover thee with My hand while I pass by: And I will take away Mine hand, and thou shalt see My back parts: but My face shall not be seen."

We all know that Moses was a very close friend of God. The Word of God records, "And the Lord spake unto Moses face to face, as a man speaketh unto his friend." Ex. 33:11.

This friendship and intimacy that Moses had with the Lord, we all can also have.

What is this rock that hides those who are near to the Lord? In Deut. 32:3, 4 we read, "Ascribe ye greatness unto our God. He is the rock." David said in Psa. 18:2. "The Lord is my rock."

The reason that God put Moses in the rock was because Moses had beseeched God that He might shew him His glory. Ex. 33:18.

The secret of this verse in the S. of S. is that the cleft of the rock is a hidden place in God where He reveals His glory to the few who say with Moses, "I beseech Thee, shew me Thy glory."

Were there not many faithful followers of God in the camp of Israel? Yet only Moses, because of his hunger and yearning for God, was hidden in the cleft of the rock, and there was revealed to him the glory of God.

> He hideth my soul in the cleft of the rock
> That shadows a dry, thirsty land;
> He hideth my life in the depth of His love.
> And covers me there with His hand
> And covers me there with His hand.

"IN THE SECRET PLACES OF THE STAIRS."

"STAIRS" can also in this instance be translated as in Eze. 38:20 — steep places, or towers.

In the days of the writing of this verse, towers were used as a place in warfare from which to fight and also as a refuge of safety. Many towers had secret hiding places.

In times of turmoil, when Satan wars against our soul and seeks to destroy our Christian testimony and to take away our very salvation, we have a refuge in God; "He is the tower of salvation" ll Sam 22:51. These were the last words that David spoke (23:1). If king David needed to seek refuge in the tower of salvation, how surely do we need to flee to Him and hide away in secret places in Christ Jesus!

In Psa. 61:3, we read that He is a strong tower from the enemy of our souls.

"LET ME SEE THY COUNTENANCE", "AND THY COUNTENANCE IS COMELY."

So many Christians never lift up their faces to the Lord. It is good to bow our heads in His presence; it is an act of humility. But the Lord would also like us to lift our faces to Him and give Him a great, big smile.

He says to you, "Let me see thy countenance for thy countenance is lovely." He loves to look at us, and when we lift our faces to Him, we are beautiful to Him.

When Moses saw the Lord face to face, it caused his face to shine. Many Christians have never left the presence of God, the place of prayer, with a shining face, the glow of salvation, because they have never learned to lift their faces up to the Lord, to allow Him to let His glory shine down upon them and be stamped upon their faces.

"I will lift up mine eyes" the psalmist says. There is a time for us to bow our heads, but there is a time to literally lift up our eyes and face towards the Lord of Hosts.

"LET ME HEAR THY VOICE, FOR SWEET IS THY VOICE."

Prayer time. Praise time. Just think! The Lord loves to hear our voice. It is sweet to Him. How many know how to pray! How few know how to praise! How many like to pray! How few like to praise!

I believe that the Lord should hear more words of praise from our lips than words of prayer.

Some say, "I praise Him in my heart; I do not need to praise Him audibly; He knows my heart." It is plain to see that the person who speaks so ignorantly, is one who is not a close friend to God. He doesn't know the thing God desires of him.

God says, "Let Me hear thy voice!" He does not say, "I am satisfied with looking at your heart. You can talk about anything you like, but you don't need to talk about Me or to Me."

Radio announcers are not chosen for their handsome looks or their physique. They are chosen for the quality of their voice. They must be pleasant to hear. As their voice goes out over the air, they must have that ability to make people want to listen to them when they speak.

What is there in your voice, as it goes out through the air, up, up into the blue sky, and is carried into the presence of God? Do you have the ability to make God listen to you? Open up your mouth to praise Him, and He will turn a listening ear your way. Your voice will be sweet to Him, when you praise His name.

vs. 15. "TAKE US THE FOXES, THE LITTLE FOXES, THAT SPOIL THE VINES: FOR OUR VINES HAVE TENDER GRAPES."

Foxes are not very dangerous animals, but they are known for their craftiness.

The Lord warns His bride to beware of these sly, little, underhand things that come into the life of a Christian and eat away at the vine.

Jesus said, "I am the vine, ye are the branches: Abide in me, and I in you. As the branch cannot bear fruit of itself, except it abide in the vine; no more can ye, except ye abide in me." John 15:5, 4.

The bridegroom is warning us about the small things that seem unimportant, which, nevertheless, eat at the vine and thus kill the branches. It is for us to be careful, to watch, lest we allow these seemingly unimportant things to break our communion with God.

"FOR OUR VINES HAVE TENDER GRAPES."

Already He sees the fruit we are bearing; He would jealously guard it from danger. How precious are these tender grapes, the fruit of the vine, which we bear because we abide in Him!

vs. 16. "MY BELOVED IS MINE, AND I AM HIS: HE FEEDETH AMONG THE LILIES."

What lilies? The lilies that grow among the thorns. Vs. 2:2.

He comes down and walks amongst us even though we grow among the thorns of life.

How good it is to feel that He belongs to us! We belong to Him. He is mine. I have fellowship with Him because He is mine. I have His love because He is mine. I possess Him.

He also possesses us. He has our fellowship because we are His. He has my love because I am His.

> Make me a captive, Lord,
> And then I shall be free;
> Force me to render up my sword,
> And I shall conqueror be.
> I sink in life's alarms
> When by myself I stand;
> Imprison me within Thine arms
> And strong shall be my hand.
>
> My heart is weak and poor
> Until it master find:
> It has no spring of action sure —
> It varies with the wind:
> It cannot freely move
> Till Thou has wrought its chain;
> Enslave it with Thy matchless love
> And deathless it shall reign.

> My will is not my own
> Till Thou hast made it Thine;
> If it would reach a monarch's throne
> It must its power resign
> It only stands unbent
> Amid the clashing strife,
> When on Thy bosom it has leant,
> And found in Thee its life.

> *George Matheson, 1890.*

True belonging means resignation of all of ones own will and desires.

When we have found the secret of the power of yieldedness, we can say, "My beloved is mine, and I am His."

vs. 17. "UNTIL THE DAY BREAK, AND THE SHADOWS FLEE AWAY, TURN, MY BELOVED, AND BE THOU LIKE A ROE OR A YOUNG HART UPON THE MOUNTAINS OF BETHER."

There is no clue as to what these mountains actually were, but they are no doubt the same mountains as mentioned in Vs. 8.

Again the bride longs for the long night of waiting to be past. She longs for the daybreak when He shall come for her. All the shadows will flee away at His coming.

Again, she calls for Him to come like the roe or hart. "Come quickly my beloved" is what she means.

CHAPTER THREE

vs. 1. "BY NIGHT ON MY BED I SOUGHT HIM WHOM MY SOUL LOVETH: I SOUGHT HIM, BUT I FOUND HIM NOT."

During the middle ages the church of Christ went through her darkest hours. But thanks be to God that in her darkest hour she was suddenly awakened to her need of the power and presence of God.

Not only to the church as a whole have come these times of spiritual darkness, but to each individual member of the church, to you, and to myself, have come times of waywardness and spiritual conflicts. Out of these "nights of darkness" we have suddenly awakened from our indifference, to realise how empty our lives are without the touch and blessing of God upon our souls.

"I SOUGHT HIM BUT I FOUND HIM NOT" reminds us of the time Samson, not realizing he had lost his power with God said, "I will go out as at other times, and shake myself. And he wist not that the Lord was departed from Him." Judges 16:20.

How long the bridegroom had been absent from the bride before she awakened to realise that the Lord had departed from her, we do not know, nor can we always look back and point out the exact place where the presence of the Lord went from us.

Not only has the presence of the Lord left individuals at times, but often we have met with different churches and organizations where one could weep for the realization that the bride in that place is sleeping on her bed of indifference, not realizing that the Lord has left her side, and the Holy Spirit has lifted from her.

"Wherefore He saith, AWAKE thou that sleepest, and arise from the dead, and Christ shall give thee light." Eph. 5:14.

The sleeping bride is not awake to the revelation of the Lord.

vs. 2. "I WILL RISE NOW, AND GO ABOUT THE CITY
IN THE STREETS, AND IN THE BROAD WAYS
I WILL SEEK HIM WHOM MY SOUL LOVETH:
I SOUGHT HIM, BUT I FOUND HIM NOT."

Awakened to her need, the bride arises to seek Him whom
her soul loveth. How can her soul rest without the Lover of
her soul!

Oh, church of Christ, awake and seek the Lord while He
may be found; call ye upon Him while He is near.

She is looking for him in the right place. The Lord is in
Zion. The psalmist says "Sing praises to the Lord who dwelleth
in Zion." Psa. 9:11.

He is so very near, much closer than she realizes, but at
first she does not find Him, for He is waiting for her to confess
her need of Him, which she does in the next verse.

vs. 3. "THE WATCHMEN THAT GO ABOUT THE CITY
FOUND ME: TO WHOM I SAID, SAW YE HIM
WHOM MY SOUL LOVETH?"

Careless and indifferent are the watchmen, watchmen whom
God has commissioned with the care of the church. How often
the leaders of the church, the watchmen which the church has
chosen to protect Zion, have been hindrances and unable to lead
the seeking ones to Christ!

Nevertheless, she has proclaimed her need. God wants the
backslidden church and individual to confess her need of God's
power. God wants them to humble themselves in their seeking
after God.

He says in Isa. 57:15. He will revive the spirit of the humble.
Many churches haven't got revival because they are not humble
enough to confess their need and to admit that the power of
God has left them. When they see others who have the power
of God, then a spirit of pride and mockery comes upon them,
and they are even more lifted up in pride, until it becomes
more and more difficult to renew them to repentance.

vs. 4. "IT WAS BUT A LITTLE THAT I PASSED FROM THEM, BUT I FOUND HIM WHOM MY SOUL LOVETH: I HELD HIM, AND WOULD NOT LET HIM GO, UNTIL I HAD BROUGHT HIM INTO MY MOTHER'S HOUSE, AND INTO THE CHAMBER OF HER THAT CONCEIVED ME."

You see, He wasn't far away. She found Him as soon as she confessed her longing for Him.

There is great power in confession. When Daniel confessed his sins and the sins of his people near the end of the capitivity, God began to prepare a way of bringing them back to their land. Zerubbabel led them back, but Daniel was the one who prayed through for their release. He prayed the prayer that softened the heart of king Cyrus. It wasn't more than 3 years after his prayer, until the first of the Jews began to return to their land.

When Ezra confessed, with weeping, the sins of the people before the house of God, revival broke out, and people put away the heathen wives they had married, and a great turning to God began in Israel. Ezra 10.

When David had finished confessing before the Lord the sin of numbering the people, the fire fell from heaven upon the sacrifice on the Threshing Floor of Ornan. 1 Chron. 21:28.

And if we confess our sins, He is faithful and just to forgive us our sins, and to cleanse us from all unrighteousness. 1 John 1:9.

When we admit our need to each other and confess it to God, we will find Him whom our soul loveth. The church will be revived.

"If my people, which are called by my name, shall humble themselves, and pray, and seek my face, and turn from their wicked ways; then will I hear from heaven, and will forgive their sin, and will heal their land." 11 Chron. 7:14.

"I HELD HIM, AND WOULD NOT LET HIM GO."

She was so afraid to lose Him. Life had been so empty without Him.

"But ye that did cleave unto the Lord are alive every one of you this day." Deut. 4:4.

So many things seek to separate us from God, but there is eternal life for us when we will cleave to Him.

The text of Joshua's dying message was "But cleave to the Lord your God." Josh. 23:8.

"Hold that fast which thou hast, that no man take thy crown:" Rev. 3:11 were the words that Jesus spoke in His warning to the church of Thyratira and also Philadelphia.

"UNTIL I HAD BROUGHT HIM INTO MY MOTHER'S HOUSE, AND INTO THE CHAMBER OF HER THAT CONCEIVED ME."

The bride brought her beloved into the innermost recess of her life.

That is the rightful place for the Lord in our lives too. When we love Him, we open our hearts to the Lord and give Him the innermost recess of our life. Christ is the very center of our hearts, the object of our affections, the motive of our living. To the bride of Christ, He becomes her "All in All."

The Christian who does not make Christ the ruling power of his life is an unhappy Christian.

Look into the inner chamber of your heart. Does Christ sit enthroned upon your heart, or are other affections taking His rightful place? Are you content to keep Him waiting in the outer court for your invitation to come in? Christ will not force His way into your affections. It is the bride who must bring Him into the chamber of her heart.

The heart is the seat of our affections.

How about your heart? Is it right with God
That's the thing that counts today.
Is it black by sin? Is it pure within?
Could you ask Christ in today?

Friend how would you feel? If your heart were made
With a window on each side?
So that all could see not just outward charm
But detect its inward heart.

People often see you as you are outside
Jesus really knows you, for He sees inside.
How about your heart? Is it right with God?
That's the thing that counts today.

vs. 5. "I CHARGE YOU, O Y E D A U G H T E R S O F
JERUSALEM, BY THE ROES, AND BY THE
HINDS OF THE FIELD, THAT YE STIR NOT UP,
NOR AWAKE MY LOVE, TILL HE PLEASE."

How strange that the verse of 2:7 should again be repeated
by the bride.

She speaks out her fears. Ever she stands on guard for her
love. The wise Christian is the one that permits nothing to
come between him and the Lord.

The bride is in continual warfare against the enemy of her
soul. Yesterday's victory was good, but today we must also win
the victory.

Over and over again the Christian must charge all that
would separate him from the Lord to not come between him
and his Lord.

vs. 6. "WHO IS THIS THAT COMETH OUT OF THE
WILDERNESS LIKE PILLARS OF SMOKE, PER-
FUMED WITH MYRRH AND FRANKINCENSE,
WITH ALL POWDERS OF THE MERCHANT?"

In 8:5 we read 'that she is leaning upon her beloved. So
we know that this is a picture of the church, the bride of Christ.

It is a revived church, one that has awakened in the night
hours to find her need of God, who has gone out to seek Him,
has humbled herself and confessed her need, found the Lord,
and has given Him the key to her heart.

Now she comes forth out of her wilderness-experience, triumphant in the power and might of the Holy Spirit.

Always the pillar of smoke is a token of the power and presence of the Holy Spirit.

The pillar of smoke is a sign that God will give the church in the last days, as a wonder, a manifestation of her spiritual state and God's anointed presence in her midst.

Joel 2:30. "And I will shew wonders in the heavens and in the earth, blood, and fire, and pillars of smoke."

The church is coming out of her wilderness-experience in the power and might of the Holy Spirit, as a sign and a marvel to the world.

"PERFUMED WITH MYRRH AND FRANKINSENSE, WITH ALL POWDERS OF THE MERCHANT."

It was in the wilderness that God gave the children of Israel the secret ingredients to be used in the anointing oil which the priests used in the tabernacle. There, without any merchants or shops of any kind, in a miraculous way, they were able to manufacture this holy anointing oil. It is as though it was provided by the hand of God.

So with the church, she will come forth out of the world, separated from it, with the holy anointing oil upon her, making her fragrant and setting her apart unto the service of God.

And so, we see the two signs of the revived church are the pillar of smoke and the anointing with holy oil, both of which have been miraculously supplied to the bride by God Himself.

vs. 7. "BEHOLD HIS BED, WHICH• IS SOLOMON'S; THREESCORE VALIANT MEN ARE ABOUT IT, OF THE• VALIANT OF ISRAEL."

The bed of Solomon was the resting place of the king. It was surrounded with the bravest soldiers of Israel, men who were especially chosen to protect the king when he was sleeping.

Why should there be threescore valiant men? Because we read there were threescore queens. 6:8.

It is as though each one of these guards were there to protect each of the queens who shared the bed with Solomon.

Now, we know that this has a greater spiritual depth of meaning. Let us therefore, with the help of the Lord, see what the Lord has for us in this portion of scripture and the following ones.

We have the privilege of being a queen. Esther is a fitting picture of a humble maiden, chosen to be the queen because of her humility in that she required nothing but what Hegai, the king's chamberlain, the keeper of the women, appointed.

Out of this group of virgins, one was chosen as the queen.

In God's kingdom, many of His children are "Queens" who have found special favour and power with the Lord.

Each one of these have dared to risk their lives for the call of God and have "sold themselves out" for God. They have, as it were, said with Esther, "If I perish, I perish." And they overcame him (Satan) by the blood of the Lamb, and by the word of their testimony; and they loved not their lives unto death. Rev. 12:11.

"He that loseth his life for My sake shall find it." Matt. 10:39.

And so we see God has put a special wall of protection around these "queens".

Who are these guardians of the queen? I believe that the guards represent the guardian angels of the queens.

As we are allowed to rest in the Lord, we are protected and surrounded by the most valiant of the angels of heaven.

vs. 8. "THEY ALL HOLD SWORDS, BEING EXPERT IN WAR: EVERY MAN HATH HIS SWORD UPON HIS THIGH BECAUSE OF FEAR IN THE NIGHT."

No doubt Solomon lived in danger of assasination as many kings of his day. But in the midst of danger there was a resting place of safety, a wall of protection.

Surely the angels are "expert in war." We read in Rev. that the angels who are the armies of heaven will in the last days make war against the beast and the false prophet and their followers and cast them alive into the lake of fire. 19:14, 19, 20. Over and over again, we see the angels given great power and authority as they go forth in the name of the Lord to fight for Him and His saints.

What need we fear, when we are surrounded by such an impregnable wall of armed beings who are expert in warfare against the principalites and powers of the night (the evil darkness of Satan)! Hallelujah, surely the King's resting place, which is our resting place, our rightful place as queens, offers us complete peace.

vs. 9. "KING SOLOMON MADE HIMSELF A CHARIOT OF THE WOOD OF LEBANON."

This word "chariot" is more rightly translated "bed", for these verses are still speaking of the Christian's resting place.

First of all, we saw our resting place as a place of Safety.

Now we see that it is made of the wood of Lebanon, which tells us that it is a place of strength, a place eternal, for as we already said in vs. 1:17, that the cedars of Lebanon were not destroyed by insects.

vs. 10. "HE MADE THE PILLARS THEREOF SILVER, THE BOTTOM THEREOF OF GOLD, THE COVERING OF IT OF PURPLE, THE MIDST THERE OF BEING PAVED WITH LOVE, FOR THE DAUGHTERS OF JERUSALEM."

"THE PILLARS OF SILVER" are the bedposts that hold up the bed. The whole foundation of our faith is the redemption He provided for us on the Cross.

Our resting place in Christ is held together by the pillars of His redeeming grace. Christ redeemed us from the curse. Gal. 3:13.

We sing praises unto Him now, and through eternity our song will be, "Thou has redeemed us to God by thy blood out of every kindred, and tongue, and people, and nation." Rev. 5:9.

"GOD will redeem my soul from the power of the grave." Psa. 49:15. All around is danger and fear, and death, but the souls that are hid in Christ are resting on the bed of redemption, safe from all danger, death, or fear.

"THE BOTTOM THEREOF OF GOLD."

Our resting place is in the very deity of the Godhead. Hallelujah! Col. 2:9. "For in Him dwelleth all the fullness of the Godhead bodily."

Christ dwelling in us, we are imparted with the power of God, the Father; God, the Son; and God, the Holy Spirit.

Truly, we are complete in Him.

We rest upon the deity of God, and not upon any righteousness of our own.

"THE COVERING OF IT OF PURPLE."

Royalty! The King has covered us with His Royalty!

> When clothed in His brightness
> Transported I rise
> To meet Him in clouds in the sky,
> His perfect salvation, His wonderful love,
> I'll shout with the millions on high.

> — *F. Crosby*

As we rest in our resting place, we are covered with His royal colour of purple.

Tyrian purple, which is a deep crimson, was used by the ancients. The dye was obtained from a shellfish found in the Mediterranean Sea. Since this shellfish yielded only a small quantity of dye, the color was very expensive. One pound of wool cost $175. Because of that, it was the symbol of rulers of wealth.

Our Lord has covered us with the symbol of His wealth, the riches in Glory by Christ Jesus.

"THE MIDST THEREOF PAVED WITH LOVE."

Gold is wonderful and priceless, but how hard it would be to sleep on a bed of gold. But, oh the Lord has made it soft with His Love. His tender, comforting love is the actual mattress upon which we lie.

A mother's arms are softened for the baby with her love.

Life is made easier for us because of God's great love for us.

His love is under you; He calls you to the resting place which He has made for you Himself. He beckons you to come and rest in His love.

The bed Solomon made was extremely large, for it was possible for 60 men to stand around it. So our resting place in God is boundless.

> For the love of God is broader
> Than the measures of man's mind
> And the heart of the Eternal
> Is most wonderfully kind

> But we make His love too narrow
> By false limits of our own;
> And we magnify His strictness
> With a zeal He will not own

F. W. Faber, 1862.

"FOR THE DAUGHTERS OF JERUSALEM."

God first extended His plan of redemption to Israel. "He came unto His own, and His own received Him not." John 1:11.

As the chosen people of the Lord, they had the first privilege of entering into the Lord's rest which He provided for them out of the Love of His heart, through the giving of His own dear Son to die for their sins. Because of the hardness of their hearts, they rejected His plan of rest for their souls.

We read in Heb. 3:19 that they could not enter into their rest because of unbelief.

"Let us therefore fear, lest, a promise being left us of entering into this rest, any of you should seem to come short of it." Heb. 4:1.

"For we which have believed do enter into rest" 4:3.

vs. 11. "GO FORTH, O YE DAUGHTERS OF ZION, AND BEHOLD KING SOLOMON WITH THE CROWN WHEREWITH HIS MOTHER CROWNED HIM IN THE DAY OF HIS ESPOUSALS, AND IN THE DAY OF THE GLADNESS OF HIS HEART."

The challenge goes out to the daughters of Zion to behold the King.

Zechariah caught the same vision when he cried, "Rejoice greatly, O daughter of Zion; shout, O daughter of Jerusalem: behold, thy King cometh unto thee: he is just and having salvation; lowly, and riding upon an ass, and upon a colt, the foal of an ass." 9:9.

We know this prophecy was actually fulfilled as is recorded in Mat. 21:5. "Tell ye the daughter of Zion, Behold, thy King cometh unto thee, meek, and sitting upon an ass, and a colt the foal of an ass."

Although they did not recognise Jesus as their King, their Messiah, the day is coming when the children of Israel, the daughters of Zion will Look upon Him whom they have pierced. Zech. 12:10.

"Behold, He cometh with clouds; and every eye shall see Him, and they also which pierced Him." Rev. 1:7.

What a glorious day that will be when the daughters of Zion will accept Jesus as their Messiah and King!

"IN THE DAY OF HIS ESPOUSALS."

Espousal means marriage or betrothal.

In Isa. 62:5 we read more about the day of Christ's espousal with Israel. "As a young man marrieth a virgin, so shall thy sons marry thee: and as the bridegroom rejoiceth over the bride, so shall thy God rejoice over thee."

We think so much about the Marriage supper of the Lamb, when He will be united with the bride. But the day when He will be united with the Daughters of Zion will also be a day of His rejoicing.

"THE DAY OF THE GLADNESS OF HIS HEART."

This entire verse seems to be the cry of the bride to the daughters of Zion. The true bride of Christ longs to see Israel turn to God and recognise Jesus Christ as their Messiah.

CHAPTER FOUR

vs. 1. "BEHOLD, THOU ART FAIR, MY LOVE: BEHOLD, THOU ART FAIR; THOU HAST DOVES' EYES WITHIN THY LOCKS: THY HAIR IS AS A FLOCK OF GOATS, THAT APPEAR FROM MOUNT GILEAD."

Chapter three was entirely the words of the bride. Now begins the beautiful description by the Bridegroom of His love and admiration for the bride. The entire chapter except for the last verse is the words of the Bridegroom.

"BEHOLD THOU ART FAIR, BEHOLD THOU ART FAIR."

Once again we hear the "Verily, verily" of the Lord as He looks in admiration upon His bride. The repetition of His words gives it power.

He spoke once, and the worlds were created. But in His love for us, He repeats His praise to us. How much then, should we repeat our words of praise and glory to Him.

"THOU HAST DOVE'S EYES WITHIN THY LOCKS."

As in 1:14 the Lord comments on the beauty of the bride's eyes. The dove is the bird of peace and tenderness.

It was said of Leah that she was tender-eyed. That is the only description that was given us of Leah, and yet it commands our admiration. There is just something about that description of her that makes us feel pity and love for Leah. Leah was the true bride of Jacob (Israel). So as the true bride of the Lord we bear the same likeness.

The eyes are the windows of the soul. If the Holy Spirit, the dove of peace, has filled our soul, then our actions should betray His innermost presence within us.

It is as though the bride of Christ sees through the eyes of the Holy Spirit.

— 59 —

Chapter 4: 1

Eyes usually speak of Spiritual discernment; and the Spirit-filled Christian sees and discerns by the power of the Holy Spirit the things of God.

Paul's prayer for the bride of Christ was that she might be filled with the knowledge of His will in all wisdom and spiritual understanding." Col. 1:9.

How beautiful then that the bride should be pictured as having doves' eyes, representing spiritual insight!

"WITHIN THY LOCKS."

The locks, the hair, as we mentioned before speak of power.

The secret of the bride's spiritual insight lies in the power of the Holy Spirit.

"THY HAIR AS A FLOCK OF GOATS THAT APPEAR FROM MOUNT GILEAD."

Gilead was a mountainous region, west of Jordon. It is first mentioned in Gen. 31:21, 25 as being the place to which Jacob fled when running away from Laban and where Laban caught up with him.

Gilead and Mt. Gilead are the same place. It was divided: half to the Reubenites and Gadites, and the other half to the half-tribe of Manasseh. Deut. 3:12, 13. It was given to the Reubenites and Gadites because they had a very great multitude of cattle, and when they saw that Gilead was a good place for cattle grazing, they asked Moses to give them their inheritance on that side of Jordan. Num. 32:1, 5.

It was known from the time of Joseph for its precious balm, which was used for healing ointment and was worth twice its weight in silver. When the brothers of Joseph were wondering what to do with their brother, they happened to see a company of Ishmaelites coming from Gilead with their camels bearing spicery and balm and myrrh, going to carry it down to Egypt. Gen. 37:25.

It is no doubt that the gifts of balm and myrrh which the children of Jacob took down into Egypt for Joseph came from Mt. Gilead, which was near to where Jacob lived. Gen. 43:11.

The healing balm of Gilead was sufficient for all the needs of Israel. It could even have been a health center in the days of Jeremiah, where physicians treated the sick. Jer. 8:22, 46:11.

The Lord said in Psa. 60:7, "Gilead is mine."

This balm came from the trees of that part of the country.

There is no doubt that the goats, when grazing upon the mountains of Gilead, would eat of the trees of healing. How typical of a goat to pull at the branches of the trees, whereas cattle only eat the grasses of the field!

Why then should the bride be likened unto the goats that feed upon Mount Gilead?

Even as the goats had found the source of the balm of Gilead, so the church in the fullness of power will not lack in God's abundant supply of healing power.

The church that is endued with power from on high has found the secret of the source of healing balm not only for herself, but she is able to send abroad to other countries; in missions of mercy she brings healing to the nations.

The words "THAT APPEAR FROM MOUNT GILEAD" are in some versions translated, "THAT EAT FROM MOUNT GILEAD" — and I would say that the latter is a more correct translation, as the secret of power is in "Eating" of the health giving trees.

> There is a balm in Gilead,
> To make the wounded whole
> There is a balm in Gilead
> To heal the sin sick soul.

vs. 2. "THY TEETH ARE LIKE A FLOCK OF SHEEP THAT ARE EVEN SHORN, WHICH CAME UP FROM THE WASHING; WHEREOF EVERY ONE BEAR TWINS, AND NONE IS BARREN AMONG THEM."

We have heard so much about the "Colgate Smile", and we all know that the most lovely face is often disappointing when the smile shows a mouth with broken, blackened or missing teeth.

There are so many different kinds of smiles. The smile of scorn and mockery, contempt, amusement, pleasure, friendship and joy.

The smile that brings response is the smile of friendship and joy. A whole-hearted smile causes the giver to show his teeth.

The smile of the bride is one of complete relaxation of the features of her face in pleasure and joy.

The smile with a perfect set of teeth is not marred by ugliness. The smile of the Christian should not be marred by the root of bitterness, or any other ugliness and sin in the heart.

What kind of an expression does your smile reveal? Is it one of worry? Hatred? Self-pity?

We have heard about "long-faced Christians". The Bride of the Song of Songs was no such person. She was a smiling, happy, radiant, joyous person.

vs. 3. "THY LIPS ARE LIKE A THREAD OF SCARLET, AND THY SPEECH IS COMELY: THY TEMPLES ARE LIKE A POMEGRANATE WITHIN THY LOCKS."

We can trace the thread of scarlet right through the Bible. Always it is a token of redemption. It speaks of the blood of Jesus Christ.

The lips of the bride of Christ speak forth that which is dearest to her heart.

Oh, the Blood, the precious Blood!
That Jesus shed for me,
Upon the cross, in crimson flood,
Just now by faith I see.

Rev. W. McDonald

Even as the lips of a dying person turn white and pale in death, so the church or denomination that loses the doctrine and message of the saving blood of Jesus, is dead and without spiritual life.

As long as the lips of the bride of Christ speak forth the message of the scarlet cord of the scriptures, she is doing that which God saved her for and called her to do.

Isaiah cried, "Woe is me! for I am undone; because I am a man of unclean lips, and dwell in the midst of a people of unclean lips:"   "Then flew one of the seraphims unto me, having a live coal in his hand, which he had taken with the tongs from off the altar: And he laid it upon my mouth, and said, Lo, this hath touched thy lips; and thine iniquity is taken away, and thy sin is purged."   6:5-7.

Prov. 10:21, "The lips of the righteous feed many."

Let us beseech God to give us lips like Isaiah had; Lips that speak forth the salvation of our God to sinners lost, and to a world in need.

"AND THY SPEECH IS COMELY."

This can be linked up with 2:14.

The Lord loves to hear us talk about Him.   There is a beautiful scripture in Mal. 3:16 which reads, "Then they that feared the Lord spake often one to another: and the Lord hearkened, and heard it, and a book of remembrance was written before Him for them that feared the Lord, and that thought upon His name."

I cannot understand Christians who do not like to talk about the things of the Lord.   Shortly after I was married, I came into a district where I found that the Christians did not like to speak about the Lord. If sometimes I mentioned the Lord, it seemed to me as though it was received with embarrassment. To this day, I can not help but wonder at it. But after many years have gone by, I have seen these same people go through great trials and spiritual conflicts, which seem to have changed them, so that now, they readily speak and even desire to speak about the things of the Lord.

The spiritual bride is one whose speech is flavoured with grace.

> Let's talk about Jesus, the King of Kings is He
> The Lord of Lords Supreme, throughout eternity,
> The Great I Am, The Way, The Truth, The Life,
>   The Door,
> Let's talk about Jesus, more and more.

"THY TEMPLES ARE LIKE A PIECE OF POMEGRANATE WITHIN THY LOCKS."

The pomegranate was the fruit of the priesthood. Worked representations of this fruit, in blue, purple and scarlet, ornamented the hem of the robe of the ephod. Ex. 28:33, 34. Its actual colour when ripe is red.

The tops of the pillars of Solomon's temple were adorned with carved figures of pomegranate. 1 Kings. 7:18, 20.

The fruit itself contains a quantity of juice which was used to make wine and medicines. It is made up of hundreds of seeds.

Because of its connection with the royal priesthood, this fruit speaks of bountiful righteousness.

Let us remember that Christ bore the crown of thorns upon His head. The thorns pierced his brow that our minds might be free from worry and anxiety. In bearing the thorny crown upon His head, He released unto us, His children, the power of casting down imaginations (or reasonings), and every high thing that exalteth itself against the Knowledge of God, and bringing into captivity every thought to the obedience of Christ. 11 Cor. 10:5.

Again we read, "Finally, brethren, whatsoever things are true, whatsoever things are honest, whatsoever things are just, whatsoever things are pure, whatsoever things are lovely, whatsoever things are of good report; if there be any virtue, and if there be any praise, think on these things." Phil. 4:8.

One of our teachers in Bible School, Mrs. Swanson, told us that God had given us the power to close the door of our mind to thoughts which were without virtue and praise.

Yes, it is true that we have this power, but the secret of its source is in the thorn-pierced brow of our blessed Saviour.

Even as the speech of the bride is comely because she speaks about the Lord, so her temples (which speak of her thoughts) are likened unto the priestly fruit, the pomegranate, for in Malachi we read again in that last part of 3:16, "And that thought upon His name."

There is such power in the Name of Jesus. Not only should we speak it in authority against the works of Satan, but we must use His Name in our thoughts as protection against the attacks of Satan upon our minds.

vs. 4. "THY NECK IS LIKE THE TOWER OF DAVID BUILDED FOR AN ARMOURY, W H E R E O N THERE HANG A THOUSAND BUCKLERS, ALL SHIELDS OF MIGHTY MEN."

There is power in obedience. As we obey God and walk in His will for our lives, we have power with God and power with man.

In Lam. 3:27 we read, "It is good for a man that he bear the yoke in his youth."

Jesus said, "Take my yoke upon you, and learn of me; for my yoke is easy, and my burden is light." Matt. 11:29a, 30.

You cannot be a true follower of Christ if you are not willing to bear His yoke. We need not fear the yoke of the Lord; He said it was an easy burden and would not be too heavy for us.

When the children of Israel refused to obey God, He called them a "stiff-necked" people.

What beauty does the Lord see in the neck of His bride? He says she is like the tower of David, a tower of strength because she bears His yoke.

What does He describe His yoke as?   A thousand bucklers. A buckler is a small round shield used for protection.   So you see, His yoke is small, and easy for us to bear.   It is not likened unto a great, heavy shield, like the shield of Goliath, and yet it is the shield of a Mighty Man.

Obedience to Christ means following Him whithersoever He leadeth us.

"Through God report and evil, Lord!
Still guided by Thy faithful Word
Our staff, our buckler, and our sword
We follow Thee.

In silence of the lonely night
In fullest glow of day's clear light
Through life's strange windings, dark or bright,
We follow Thee.

Great Master! point Thou out the way
Nor suffer Thou our steps to stray
Then in the path that leads to day,
We follow Thee.

Thou hast passed on before our face
Thy footsteps on the way we trace;
Still in Thy light we onward move,
We follow Thee."

vs. 5. "THY TWO BREASTS ARE LIKE TWO YOUNG ROES THAT ARE TWINS, WHICH FEED AMONG THE LILIES."

With this verse ends, for the time being, a description of the bride. It is as though the artist has painted only the upper part of the bride's portrait, or the sculpture has chiselled only the bust of his subject.

Later on in chapter 7, we have the completion of the portrayal, but now for a time, it closes with the description of the love and affections of the Christian.

We know that the breasts speak of love. The Love of the Christian for his Saviour then, is compared to young roes. As we said before, the roe was celebrated for its loveliness. The most beautiful thing that the Christian manifests, is his love for the Lord.

You will notice that it says, "young roes". The love of the new Christian is so lovely to see. How it thrills our hearts to see a new "babe in Christ" manifest a real love for the Lord Jesus Christ, a love that is tender as a young roe! It may be a bit timid, but it is without fear.

The Lord said to the church of Ephesus, "I have somewhat against thee, because thou hast left thy first love." Rev. 2:4.

It was like the love that the Israelites had for the Lord in the wilderness, as we read in Jer. 2:2, "Thus saith the Lord; I remember thee, the kindness of thy youth, the love of thine espousals (betrothal to the Lord), when thou wentest after me in the wilderness."

"WHICH FEED AMONG THE LILES."

The love of the Christian grows stronger in the fellowship she shares with that other One who also feeds among the lilies. 2:16.

May the Love we have for the Lord always live in our hearts as fresh and as strong as when we first fell in love with Jesus.

Walking one evening with a friend in Hong Kong, we passed a young Chinese couple, who, it was plain to see, were very much in love. I turned to my friend and mentioned to her how beautiful it was to see the love they had for each other. We almost felt as though we were looking at something we had no right to see. I mentioned how it pictured our first love for the Lord.

I was shaken to my soul when she answered, "Yes Gwen, I can remember when you loved the Lord like that. Somehow it seems as though you do not love Him like I remember you used to. You have changed."

What she said made me want to deny it; it also made me feel like weeping. I thought about it over and over again for many weeks. I hadn't realized it myself, but I knew what she said was true.

What was the reason for this? I had not fed among the lilies as I should have. I had neglected my communion and fellowship with the Lord. Everything and everyone around me did not have the anointing that inspires a deeper walk with the Lord.

I sought God earnestly; I feel that when I was home again on furlough, God, through others, brought me back into close communion and fellowship with Himself.

vs. 6. "UNTIL THE DAY BREAK, AND THE SHADOWS FLEE AWAY, I WILL GET ME TO THE MOUNTAIN OF MYRRH, AND TO THE HILL OF FRANKINCENSE."

In the last verse of chapter 2 the bride expressed her longing for the return of the Lord in the same words which He now uses, but He adds that he will wait until that day at the mountain of myrrh and the hill of frankincense.

After the Lord Jesus had accomplished His work, He returned to heaven and sat down at the right hand of the Father.

Myrrh, speaks first of suffering and also of anointing. It was one of the ingredients in the "oil of holy oinitment." Ex. 30:23.

It was used in the purification of women, Esther 2:12.

It was used as a perfume, Ps. 45:8, Prov. 7:17.

It was one of the gifts brought to Jesus by the wise men.

On the cross it was mingled with wine and offered to Jesus. Mk. 15:23.

Nicodemus brought a mixture of myrrh and aloes, about a hundred pounds, to use in embalming Jesus body.

Truly our Lord suffered, even unto death. He went to the "mount of suffering" called Calvary that we might be able to draw nigh unto the "mount of His glory."

Then too, as we mentioned before, the myrrh speaks of the anointing of God. God's eternal presence is the source of all anointing and power.

From the account in Ex. 24 we will remember how God came down upon Mt. Sinai with great glory. His presence covered that mountain. The people were not allowed to touch the mount, and bounds were set up around it lest they should break through and be destroyed.

That mount of anointing was only a type of the true mountain of God's storehouse of power which is now open for us all, as we read in Heb. 12:18, "For ye are not come unto the mount that might be touched, and that burned with fire, but ye are come unto mount Zion, and unto the city of the living God, the heavenly Jerusalem and to an innumerable company of angels." vs. 22.

From that mountain of power which was made accessible to the church of Christ on the day of Pentecost, we now receive a continual supply of anointing and power.

"AND TO THE HILL OF FRANKINCENSE."

Frankincense was a sticky substance which exuded from the bark of a tree called Arbor thuris. It was brittle, glittering, and of bitter taste, used for the purpose of sacrificial fumigation. Ex. 30:34-36. Because it burned so freely and gave off its perfumed odour, it is called "frank" incense. It would burn with a steady, unflickering flame for a long time. A light that shines unfalteringly is pleasing unto God; — such should be our fragrant testimony.

Frankincense was used in the compounding of the incense which was used continually in the temple. The incense which the Lord told them how to make had to be made exactly according to directions. Of all the ingredients used, frankincense seemed to be the most important, as it is especially mentioned so many times, and sometimes was even used alone in the sacrificial offerings.

The offering of the burnt sacrifices of many animals would have caused the stench of burning flesh to spread throughout the camp without the frankincense acting as a fumigant. The frankincense becomes a symbol of the offering of Himself, together with His intercession, which makes our prayers acceptable to God.

Even as the frankincense gave off its odour freely, so we see how it pictures our Lord, who freely gave Himself.

The steadfast flame which burned steadily without going out speaks of the Lord's eternal sacrifice, as we read in Heb. 10:11, "We are sanctified through the offering of the body of Jesus Christ once for all."

He has returned to heaven to make intercession for the saints. "Seeing He ever liveth to make intercession for them." Heb. 7:25.

His finished work and His continual ministry on our behalf, therefore, is the hill of frankincense.

And so He continues His work until the day break and the shadows flee away.

vs. 7. "THOU ART ALL FAIR, MY LOVE: THERE IS NO SPOT IN THEE."

It is as though the Lord looks ahead to that morning when the shadows will flee away, and He shall gather the church to Himself. He looks at the bride of Christ and sees a glorious church, not having spot or wrinkle, or any such thing; a glorious church, holy and without blemish. Eph. 5:27.

On that fair morning He will present us to Himself.

"Do you hear them coming brother
Thronging up the steeps of light
Clad in glorious shining garments
Blood washed garments, pure and white?

'Tis a glorious church without spot or wrinkle
Washed in the blood of the Lamb."

vs. 8. "COME WITH ME FROM LEBANON, MY SPOUSE,
WITH ME FROM LEBANON: LOOK FROM THE
TOP OF AMANA, FROM THE TOP OF SHENIR
AND HERMON, FROM THE LIONS' DENS, FROM
THE MOUNTAIN, OF THE LEOPARDS."

Three different mountain names are given in this one verse.
Each one of these mountains belong to the mountain ranges
known as the mountains of Lebanon. The eastern range was
known as the mountains towards the sunrising. Josh. 13:5. The
mountains of Lebanon are two different ranges, about 90 miles
long which run parallel from the southwest to the northeast.
The name Lebanon signifies "white". It was likely called by
this name because of the snow which covers it most of the year
or because the limestone cliffs and peaks which are white in
colour.

AMANA means, "covenant". It is believed that it belonged
to the Lebanon range, and was the source of the river of Abana.

SHENIR or SENIR is the Amorite name of MOUNT
HERMON. It means "snow mountain". Mt. HERMON is the
highest mountain in the eastern range. It is the most easily seen,
as well as the most beautiful of all the mountains of Palestine.
It has three summits. As it stands near Caesarea Philippi, it is
probable that the scene of the transfiguration took place in some
part of it. The Mt. is approximately 10,000 feet high.

Why does the Lord point out these mountains to us and call us to the tops of these two different mountains of Lebanon?

Let us look more closely at the meaning of their names, "Covenant" and "Snow Mountain".

First, He calls us to the mount of His covenant, 'Amana'. The first step that we take with the Lord, if we would follow Him, is to the mount of His Covenant, which is Calvary. God said He would make a new covenant with us. Christ is the mediator of the new covenant. Heb. 12:24.

From the Mount of the Covenant, which is Calvary, He calls us to the next step which is the Mount of Snow. In Isa. 1:18 we read, "though your sins be as scarlet, they shall be white as snow." Oh, how wonderful is the experience of knowing that your soul is white as the snow, clean and pure before God! We cannot experience this, however, unless we first have met Him on the Mount of Covenant.

And then we remember the "Snow Mountain" as being the scene of the transfiguration. We read that His raiment became as snow. Matt. 28:3. This is Mount Hermon, the peak of all the mountains. The place where we learn to know Christ in all His glory. Oh, how He seeks to lead us on from Glory to Glory, until we are changed into His likeness.

Let us not stay forever at the mount of the covenant. Let us walk on in God. Let us ask and seek Him to make us one of "the three", the chosen few who follow on to know the Lord. Therefore, leaving the principles of the doctrine of Christ, let us go on unto perfection. Heb. 6:1.

From here we stand upon the highest mountain peak. This is the zenith of the Christian experience. It is also the mount that faces the east upon which the first rays of the rising sun fall. From here we await the day break. From here we shall see the shadows flee away.

Oh shadows, that would darken our lives and cast blackness upon our souls, we are free from you, when we take the hand of our Master and let Him lead us to this mountain.

"FROM THE LION'S DENS, FROM THE MOUNTAINS OF THE LEOPARDS."

The mountains of Lebanon were inhabited with many fierce animals. 11 Kings 14:9, Hab. 2:17. Even until lately there were such animals as the jackals, hyaenas, wolves, bears and panthers.

So many stay along the lower peaks of Christian experiences and never climb the heights with God. All about them are the dangers of the enemy. If we choose to walk beside the lions' dens and amidst the mountains of the leopards, our souls are endangered by Satan, who goeth about like a roaring lion, seeking whom he may devour. 1 Peter 5:8.

To the backslider and the wanderer, even God would become as a lion and a leopard to destroy them in judgement.

Hosea 13:7, 8. "Therefore I will be as a lion: as a leopard by the way will I observe them: There will I devour them like a lion; the wild beast shall tear them."

The soul that goes on in God is saved from these dangers. Let us rise to climb the mountain peaks with God.

vs. 9. "THOU HAST RAVISHED MY HEART, MY SISTER, MY SPOUSE; THOU HAST RAVISHED MY HEART WITH ONE OF THINE EYES, WITH ONE CHAIN OF THY NECK."

"Ravish", or "to carry off by force" which is a better translation. This makes one realize the tremendous powers of persuasion the bride has over her Beloved.

What is it about her eyes that compels Him to be so enraptured? It is none other than the love-light which He sees.

There is power and compelling force with Christ if the heart of the Christian is filled with love for the Lord.

A certain woman told me about someone she had loved in her girlhood. Although they had been very attached to each other, through circumstances that came into their lives they had never married. I asked her if she had ever seen him whom she had loved, in later years. "Yes", she said, "I saw him, but he never saw me. I stayed in my room upstairs when he happened to call at a house where I was staying during my holidays." I asked her why she had not gone downstairs and spoken to him. She answered me, "Because I would never have wanted him to have a chance to look into my eyes."

I have never forgotten these significant words.

What does the Lord see when He looks into your eyes, which as we said before, are the windows of your soul? Is He satisfied that you love Him more than all else? Have you set your affection on things above? Do You seek first the kingdom of God?

"WITH ONE CHAIN OF THY NECK."

These are part of the jewels of betrothal which the bridegroom gave the bride in 1:10. They are binding. Anyone who looks upon them, recognises them as a token of marriage.

There are times when the bride has removed her token of marriage and laid it aside. The removal of the wedding ring is often a sign of separation or divorce.

When the bride is first given these gifts, she wears them with love. She wants the world to know that she is loved by someone. She wears them also with pride. The size of the diamond makes very little difference to the girl who receives the gift with true love.

What have you done with your love gift from the Lord? When you received Him as your Saviour, you were married spiritually to the Lord. He gave you the golden chain of His love to wear. Where is it today? Have you lost your love for Him? Have you removed the chain and put it in the back of some drawer?

Paul says in Col. 3:14. "And above all these things, PUT ON LOVE, which is the perfect bond."

Wear your love for the Lord for all to see. Never be ashamed of loving Jesus. Love Him with pride. Tell others of His love for you.

vs. 10. "HOW FAIR IS THY LOVE, MY SISTER, MY
SPOUSE! HOW MUCH BETTER IS THY LOVE
THAN WINE! AND THE SMELL OF THINE
OINTMENTS THAN ALL SPICES!"

"HOW FAIR IS THY LOVE, MY SISTER, MY SPOUSE."

The love of the Christian for the Lord is beautiful. It is
the result of constant communion and fellowship with the Lord.

When we were in North-West China, we lived near an
elderly missionary who had spent many years on the mission
field. Most of her life she had lived apart from other people
of her race. In her hunger for companionship, she had made
the Lord her closest friend. I remember when we used to pray
together. This dear sister did not pray. She talked to the Lord
as friend to friend. One listening, could just feel the close
relationship there was between her and the Lord. It was
beautiful!

If it was beautiful to us, how much more to Him whom
she loved.

"HOW MUCH BETTER IS THY LOVE THAN WINE."

The bride said in 1:4. "We will remember thy love more
than wine."

Love endures long and is patient and kind;
Love never is envious nor boils over with jealousy;
Is not boastful or vainglorious,
Does not display itself haughtily.

It is not conceited-arrogant and inflated with pride;
It is not rude (unmannerly), and does not act
    unbecomingly;
Love, (God's love in us) does not insist on its own
    rights or its own way, for it is not self-seeking;
It is not touchy or fretful or resentful;
It takes no account of evil done to it-pays no attention
    to wrong.

It does not rejoice at injustice and unrighteousness,
    but rejoices when right and truth prevail.

Love bears up under anything and everything that comes,
Is ever ready to believe the best of every person,

Its hopes are fadeless under all circumstances and it
endures everything (without weakening).

Love never fails—never fades out or becomes obsolete or comes
to an end. 1 Cor. 13:1-8a. Amplified New Testament.

"AND THE SMELL OF THINE OINTMENTS THAN ALL SPICES!"

Looking back to 1:3 we read again "Thy name is as ointment poured forth."

Where then does the bride of Christ receive this lovely ointment that the Lord says is better than all other spices?

The supply of this ointment is in His Name. When we take on His name, which we do when we become Christians, we receive from Christ the ointment.

Ointment was used on many difference occassions.

1. Cosmetic — Ruth 3:3, we read how Ruth made herself more attractive by anointing herself.
2. Funeral — The clothes and bodies of the dead were heavily anointed. It hindered the decay of flesh. Matt. 26:12.
3. Medicinal — Ointment was used to bring healing to the sick. Some ointment was used as eye-salve. Isa. 1:6.
4. Consecration — It was used in connection with the rites of consecration. Ex. 30:30.

An apothecary was one who compounded these ointments.

Christ is the apothecary of the Christian.

1. He beautifies the soul that belongs to Him.
2. In death He keeps our soul from destruction.
3. In sickness He is the source of our healing.
4. In seeking the spiritual, He readily anoints our eyes to discern His will. Rev. 3:18.
5. When we consecrate ourselves to Him, He anoints us with the Holy Spirit.

Truly the anointing we have received with His ointment is better than all spices.

vs. 11.   "THY LIPS, O MY SPOUSE, DROP AS THE HONEYCOMB: HONEY AND MILK ARE UNDER THY TONGUE; AND THE SMELL OF THY GARMENTS IS LIKE THE SMELL OF LEBANON."

"THY LIPS, O MY SPOUSE, DROP AS THE HONEYCOMB: HONEY AND MILK ARE UNDER THY TONGUE."

Prov. 16:24. "Pleasant words are as a honeycomb, sweet to the soul, and health to the bones."

We all remember how Samson, on his way to the Philistines, came across the lion he had killed on an earlier trip. The vultures had picked clean the meat off the lion and left the empty shell of the carcass. Examining it more closely, Samson found in the carcass of the dead lion a honeycomb which he took out and ate as he went along his way. Later he made up this riddle, "Out of the strong came forth sweetness." Judges 14:14.

There is a lot of truth in these words. James in 1:26 said, "If any man among you seem to be religious, and bridleth not his tongue, but deceiveth his own heart, this man's religion is vain."

It took a strong man to kill that strong lion. He did it by the power of God. Out of the dead lion came forth sweetness in the form of the honeycomb.

It takes a strong Christian to subdue and bridle his tongue. He can conquer all evil words by the power of God. When we die to self, out of our mouths come forth words as the honeycomb, "sweet to the soul, health to the bones."

I can't think of anything as repulsive to the Christian as hearing the man in sin curse God and use vile language. It fairly makes my flesh creep, and I sometimes wonder why God does not smite such a one dead instantly.

I remember a young man who worked near me. He was strong and healthy. He married one of the girls who also worked in the same place. I went to their wedding. This young man had the vilest tongue I ever heard. He cursed God with almost every sentence he spoke. I used to wonder how God could allow him to continue in this blasphemous way. I wasn't too shocked to hear that shortly after his marriage he was suddenly seized with strange fits and died in a terrible manner. I always believed the judgment of God struck him down.

As saints of God, our mouths should speak words of sweetness, words that bring health to the bones. The "Milk" mentioned in this verse is the precious milk of the word of God. 1 Peter 2:2.

"AND THE SMELL OF THY GARMENTS IS LIKE THE SMELL OF LEBANON."

One of the most important things in the purchases of the bride-to-be is the "hope-chest." Usually, in our part of the world, it is made of cedar. In the Far East it is of camphor-wood. The chest itself is very fragrant because of the wood with which it is lined. It is always moth proof. All garments stored in it are kept in good condition for a long period of time.

No doubt the bride of Song of Songs, also kept her wardrobe in a chest made from the cedars of Lebanon. As she put on her garments, the fragrance still lingered upon them.

The Lord has given us a robe of righteousness to wear. It is a garment that fadeth not away. Moths cannot corrupt or eat holes in it. It bears the fragrance of heaven from which it hath come.

No soul can enter into heaven's gates without this wedding garment.

We may think that our own works have fashioned one that is equal in value and in beauty. But God says that it is as a filthy rag.

Each person who receives an invitation to the marriage of the king, receives a robe from the King Himself.

If we would gain entrance into the Halls of Heaven, we must come, clothed in the robe He provides, the robe of righteousness, paid for by Jesus Christ's atonement. It is priceless. It is ours. It has been purchased.

vs. 12. "A GARDEN ENCLOSED IS MY SISTER, MY SPOUSE; A SPRING SHUT UP, A FOUNTAIN SEALED."

A garden that has no wall about it is open for animals and people to come in and destroy it.

Thank God, the Lord says that we are not open for destruction. He has put a wall around us. He has sealed us off from that which would destroy and harm us.

Remember when Balaam, a prophet of God, (though he was backslidden), went forth against the will of God, the Lord protected him from destruction by putting a wall around him. Num. 22:24. As he sought to go forward, there was a wall on this side and a wall on that side, and the angel of the Lord stood in the way and would not let him pass. If the angel had not been able to stop Balaam, he would have slain him with his sword.

How many times has God had to put a wall around us to keep us from doing that which would be to our own destruction!

Once when I was seeking my own will in a certain matter, God put a wall like this around me and stopped me "dead in my tracks." I have often thanked Him. He saved me from a lot of misunderstanding and heartache.

The wall God has put around us is for our good. Sometimes we may be happy for it, because we feel the safety that lies within the walls. Other times we may feel resentful against the barriers that would hinder us from doing our own will. But let us thank God, and remember they are for our good.

When Israel backslid, God said He would break down the wall around her and allow her to be trodden down. Isa. 5:5. "And now go to; I will tell you what I will do to my vineyard:

— 79 —

I will take away the hedge thereof and it shall be eaten up; and break down the wall thereof, and it shall be trodden down:"

In Proverbs 24:30, 31, we read, "I went by the field of the slothful, and by the vineyard of the man void of understanding; and, lo, it was all grown over with thorns, and nettles had covered the face thereof, and the stone wall thereof was broken down."

vs. 12b, 15.   "A SPRING SHUT UP, A FOUNTAIN SEALED."

vs. 15.   "A FOUNTAIN OF GARDENS, A WELL OF LIVING WATERS, AND STREAMS FROM LEBANON."

I would like to join the latter part of verse 12 and all of verse 15 together as they fit more closely that way. After that we will return to verses 13 and 14.

These are four descriptive phrases which are much alike. We will study them a little more fully.

1.   "A SPRING SHUT UP", ("A SPRING ENCLOSED)." "A FOUNTAIN SEALED," ("A FOUNTAIN ENCLOSED)."

The Hebrew for the words "shut up" is "barred". It carries the same meaning as garden "enclosed". (vs. 12)

A spring and a fountain are the same thing. They are a source of supply, an issue of water from the earth.

The springs of Palestine were usually only short-lived, but they were outstanding for their abundance and also for their beauty. There were hundreds along the Jordan river and surrounding the lakes. In the city of Jerusalem there was one or more perennial springs.

The importance of the springs and fountains of the earth can never be over-estimated. Though they are small and often hidden away in far away, inaccessible places, still they are the source of the mighty rivers of the earth. They are found in hills, mountains and valleys. They are usually ice cold, but can be warm or hot, as we find in such places as the Yellowstone

National Park, U.S.A. They may have good tasting water, or they may be poisonous as the spring at Jericho which Elisha healed by casting salt into it. 11 Kings 2:21. Some springs contain strong minerals which are used as healing baths for the sick.

The fountain springing up out of the dry earth or rocks, brings life to all that it contacts as it flows through the land. Many countries depend on these sources for the water-supply in irrigating the land.

In Isa. 58:11. The Lord says, "And thou shalt be like a watered garden, and like a spring of water, whose waters fail not." This is a perennial spring. It is everlasting because it is connected with the ETERNAL supply.

Some springs dry up because of lack of rain. But we read in Psalm. 87:7, "All my springs are in Thee."

You are the Lord's "spring". He has placed you in a dry and needy land that you might be a source of blessing where you are most needed. He has placed you in the right place just as surely as he placed the fountains of the land. Psa. 104:10. "He sendeth the springs into the valleys, which run among the hills." Read on in the verses that follow, and you will be surprised just how powerful are the affects of these springs which He has placed in the valleys.

1. They give drink to the beasts.
2. Beside them the birds have their nests built, and sing their song.
3. The hills are watered.
4. They cause the grass to grow for the cattle.
5. They bring forth Herbs for the need of man.
6. They supply food for all the earth.
7. They supply the wine to make glad the heart.
8. They furnish oil to make his face to shine.
9. They provide bread to strengthen his body.

All of us were dry land before we were saved. Some of us were even hard rock. But when God saved our souls He turned us into springs. The fountains of the deep were opened in our souls. ("He turneth the wilderness into a standing water, and dry ground into watersprings." Psa. 107:35).

It is good to see people weep their way through to the Lord in old-fashioned repentance. You can almost see the Lord breaking the rock open, that the waters of the fountain may gush forth. "Psa. 74:15. "Thou 'didst cleave the fountain." Truly, only God can break up the hard heart of man.

Never be ashamed of the tears you weep when God's Spirit moves upon you. Remember He is cleaning the fountain.

2. "A WELL OF LIVING WATERS."

A well differs a little from the fountain and spring in that it is not only an issue of water from the earth, but it has an accompanying pool. Sometimes a well is a hole sunk into the earth to reach a water supply farther down which would otherwise never be seen.

Water can sometimes be reached by digging only a few feet below the surface, but the water is not good and may even be dangerous.

The deeper the well is, the purer is the water. In dry places the wells often have to go down many feet before the supply is found. Nearly every good well is at least 20 feet deep.

WHAT kind of a well are you? How much have you allowed the Holy Spirit to dig out of your life? Have you been content with the first few feet of digging? Or have you allowed God to search your soul and dig deep into your life to remove the soil and the filth that you may be a healthy well of water?

There are three levels of water in digging a well. The first one, (which is called the watertable), is unhealthy, and so diggers always dig below until they strike the second level. Many Christians stop at the first. Most of us stop at the second level. But friend, there is a third level, — far, far down. It is below a layer of hard rock. But when it is reached, it becomes an artesian well. It sprouts up without the aid of pumping, because it is under pressure.

Most of us need continual pumping to be a blessing in this world. That is because we have not let God dig deeper into our lives, through the hard layer of rock. We have not completely died to self.

Jesus said to the woman at the well. "The water that I shall give him shall be in him a well of water springing up into everlasting life." John. 4:14.

This is the artesian well. It needs no pumping. It springs up from the deep because of the pressure it has within itself, the mighty force of the power of the Holy Spirit.

The woman did not understand this. She said to the Lord, "Sir, thou hast nothing to draw with, and the well is deep; from whence then hast thou that living water?" 4:11.

But we don't need any vessel to draw from this well. It is the artesian well. That is the well that was in our Lord. There was no uncleanness in Him. There was no hard layer of rock in Him. He had the fullness of God's Spirit dwelling in Him.

But the wonderful thing is that if we will allow God to dig in our lives, we can reach that place too. He told her, that the water He would give her would be a well of water springing up.

Oh, brother and sister, let's dig a little deeper.

3.   "AND STREAMS FROM LEBANON."

A stream is a current, or course of water, flowing in the earth. Larger streams are known as rivers.

The streams that came down from the mountains of Lebanon did not always stay streams; they turned into lakes and finally into the river Jordan. The source of the Jordan river came from the springs and streams that flowed down the slopes of Mount Hermon. First the streams fall sharply to Lake Hula, then run a short distance of ten miles before filling the sea of Galilee and the river Jordan, and then empty into the Dead Sea.

When the snows melted on Mount Hermon, the streams became rushing torrents that caused Jordan to flood over its banks. During the dry season the river Jordan was sometimes only 5 feet deep.

What about you? Have you gone with the Lord to Mount Hermon as He called you in 4:8? If you have, then the source of your stream is in the highest mountain. You shall flow into the river Jordan.

"He that believeth in Me, as the scripture hath said, out of his belly shall flow rivers of living water. And this spake He of the Spirit, which they that believe on Him should receive: for the Holy Ghost was not yet given." John 7:38, 39.

We can never become as the streams from Lebanon until we have been filled with the blessed Holy Spirit.

Before leaving this verse let us look at Isa. 41:17, 18. "When the poor and needy seek water, and there is none, and their tongue faileth them for thirst, I the Lord will hear them, I the God of Israel will not forsake them."

— I will open rivers in high places (STREAMS FROM LEBANON).

— and fountains in the midst of the valleys: (A FOUNTAIN ENCLOSED, A FOUNTAIN OF GARDENS):

— I will make the wilderness a pool of water, (A WELL OF LIVING WATER WITH ITS ACCOMPANYING POOL).

— and the dry land, springs of water (A SPRING ENCLOSED).

How remarkable that this verse in Isaiah should use the same comparisons as that in the Song of Songs!

Today the world is dry and parched. Many thirsty souls are crying out for water. God promises He will open up

> — rivers in the mountains
> — fountains in the valleys
> — wells with pools in the wilderness
> — springs and fountains in the dry land.

In the year 1907 a prophetic vision was given to Mrs. Rachel Sizelove. Today, over fifty years later we see the fulfillment of that which God revealed to her. What was the remarkable vision that she had?   Seven years before there was born the great denomination called The Assemblies of God, she saw in Springfield, Missouri, by the revelation of God, a mighty fountain of water springing up in the heart of this city.   It was not until eleven years later that the Assemblies of God headquarters moved into this city.   Even as she saw in the vision, this fountain as the source of many great rivers of blessing, flowing out to the ends of the earth, we can today look around us in any of the far and distant corners of the world and see Bible schools, churches, printing presses, missionaries and native preachers who have their source in this organization which has been so greatly blessed of God.   Mrs. Sizelove, a Holiness evangelist, was the source of this great fountain for she brought the Pentecostal message to Springfield.

Oh, Hallelujah, will you and I let Him turn us into these mighty sources of power and blessing to those in need?

vs. 13,14. "THY PLANTS ARE AN ORCHARD OF POMEGRANATES, WITH PLEASANT FRUITS; CAMPHIRE, WITH SPIKENARD, SPIKENARD AND SAFFRON: CALAMUS AND CINNAMON, WITH ALL TREES OF FRANKINCENSE; MYRRH AND ALOES, WITH ALL THE CHIEF SPICES:"

You will remember that in verse 12 the Lord described the bride of Christ as a garden that was enclosed.   Now He tells us what is inside this garden.

"AN ORCHARD OF POMEGRANATES WITH PLEASANT FRUITS."

The pomegrante, as we said when discussing 4:3, is the fruit of the priesthood and spoke of righteousness.   The bride's garden has a whole orchard of righteous fruits.   It is mentioned first of all, showing its great importance.

God has planted in us the trees of righteousness that we might produce the fruit of righteousness which is Peace.   Heb. 12:11.

"CAMPHIRE"

The camphor tree grows tall and has white flowers and green leaves. Camphor is taken from branches of the camphor tree by steaming them until they give off drops of camphor as if they were perspiring.

Standing in the orchard, they look lovely. But there is suffering in store for them. The branches are cut off, and the heat is applied until they produce, until they give off the substance that is so needed in the world.

Although we now have synthetic camphor, in Bible days, the only supply came from the camphor tree.

There come times of suffering in our lives. Times of hot persecution when it seems as though our life is being drained from us. We may not see the good in it. But remember God is getting from our life that which otherwise would always be hidden and useless.

"SPIKENARD"

Spikenard was a herb. It was ointment from this herb that Mary used to anoint the Lord as He sat at meat in Simon's house. It would cost hundreds of dollars to purchase that amount that Mary used if reckoned at the wages of laborers today.

Out of our lives come forth that which is very precious, that which can be used to bring fragrance and anointing.

"SAFFRON"

Saffron is a kind of crocus in the iris family. From the earliest times it has been highly valued as a perfume.

It is also used as a flavour for cooking. It is a brilliant yellow dye.

About 4,000 flowers yield one ounce of saffron.

"CALAMUS"

A reed. It seems that it produced a seed much like corn.

It certainly speaks of that which is plain in our lives.   There are so many ordinary days.   So much that is "hum-drum" in our lives.   Yet God wants us to realise we still have our feet planted on the earth.

"CINNAMON"

The cinnamon laurel tree grows as high as 20 - 30 feet.   It has tiny pale-yellow flowers.   Usually the trees that are in use are kept small.   The bark is peeled for the use of making cinnamon.   It is pleasant tasting and also has a nice odour.

Some of the trees in the garden are useful because of their fruit — i.e. the pomegranate.

The Camphor tree has its hidden value deep within its branches.

The cinnamon comes from the bark.

God has many different ways of receiving glory from His church which is the garden.

"TREES OF FRANKINCENSE"

These might be any of a number of certain trees of East Africa and Arabia.

We will remember that we mentioned it was the gum-resin that was used from these trees to make incense.   It is sold in the form of pale-colored globules called "tears."   It has been used for embalming, fumigating and making incense.

The tree has to be cut before the resin can flow out.

Many times we suffer pains and injuries from others by the hand of God that our lives might produce a sweet frankincense before the Lord.

"MYRRH"

Certain shrubs of Eastern Africa and Arabia give off a fragrant gumlike substance which is called myrrh.   It has a bitter taste, which probably explains its name.   The Greek word, myrrha, means bitter.

It was one of the ingredients of the oil of holy ointment. It was used in the purification of women.

On the cross it was offered to the Lord, mingled with wine. Mark 15:23.

It seems strange that anointing and bitterness are linked together, and that there should be that which is bitter included in the anointing oil.

Perhaps it speaks of the cross that comes with the anointing of God upon one's life.

Often we see people who shine with the anointing of God upon them like oil, yet we do not know the bitterness of myrrh which they may have suffered to attain their priceless treasure.

"ALOES"

Aloes is the name of a group of about one hundred fleshy, leaved plants of warm countries, especially South Africa. Aloe plants range in height from a few inches to 30 feet or more. The leaves are very large. The flowers are in clusters of yellow or red, and are tube shaped.

The leaves have a bitter juice which is dried by evaporation and used in medicine. It is good for the liver.

The fibers in the large leaves are used for cordage, fishing nets, and coarse cloth. Others have a finer fiber which can be made into lace. Some leaves produce a lovely violet dye.

We see that God has planted in our garden the aloe which is healing, which is useful and needed, and which speaks again of royalty.

The value of the aloe is in its leaves.

Each one of the trees mentioned, produces its treasure in some different way. We are all different, and God has made us differently for a purpose. In one He sees this which He can use, in another He sees that. In still another, He sees still some other quality.

Whether it be that we are valued for the flower, the leaf, the root, the resin, the bark, or the branch, makes little difference.

Only may He find some part in each one of us which He will find useful for the extention of His kingdom and for His honour and glory.

"AND WITH ALL THE CHIEF SPICES."

Lest some tree of signifigrance or some herb or shrub of usefulness be left out, he finally adds, "all the chief spices." Truly in the garden of the Lord, are all trees precious.

Most of these trees mentioned and shrubs and plants, were not grown in Palestine. Therefore, it is impossible or at least very unlikely, that any literal garden is meant by these two verses. This makes us realize that the language is figurative and is a picture of that which is spiritual, just as all of the Song of Songs is meant to be.

vs. 16. "AWAKE, O NORTH WIND; AND COME, THOU SOUTH; BLOW UPON MY GARDEN, THAT THE SPICES THEREOF MAY FLOW OUT. LET MY BELOVED COME INTO HIS GARDEN, AND EAT HIS PLEASANT FRUITS."

"AWAKE OF NORTH WIND AND COME, THOU SOUTH;"

The bride of the garden calls out, "Come trials, come persecutions, let the winds of the cold winter, the hot winds of the summer blow upon me, for when you blow, you will pick up the fragrance of my trees and carry it with you to places beyond."

"LET MY BELOVED COME INTO HIS GARDEN AND EAT HIS PLEASANT FRUITS."

It takes the different seasons of the year to perfect and ripen the fruit of the garden. It takes the hard places in our lives to make us ready and perfect so that He may come in and eat of His pleasant fruits.

God may be in the wind. So do not fear when it blows its cold breath against your face. Remember the song of David. 11 Sam. 22:11, "He was seen upon the wings of the wind."

CHAPTER FIVE

vs. 1. "I AM COME INTO MY GARDEN, MY SISTER, MY SPOUSE: I HAVE GATHERED MY MYRRH WITH MY SPICE; I HAVE EATEN MY HONEYCOMB WITH MY HONEY; I HAVE DRUNK MY WINE WITH MY MILK: EAT, O FRIENDS; DRINK, YEA, DRINK ABUNDANTLY, O BELOVED."

"I AM COME INTO MY GARDEN, MY SISTER, MY SPOUSE:"

Notice the past tenses in this verse.

I "am" come - - -
I "have" gathered - - -
I "have" eaten - - -
I "have" drunk - - -

In the last verse of ch. 4 we read the invitation of the bride which she extended to the Lord, beseeching Him to come into her garden, which you may notice she calls "his" garden, even though in vs. 13, 14, He spoke as though it was her garden.

Everything that we possess has been given us by the Lord and we have given it back to Him in dedication and consecration. He gave her the garden, He planted it for her, and now she has called Him to come into His garden.

He accepts her token of love and says, "I have come into "My" garden."

There is a two-fold meaning in this verse. The first one as we see it, is the Lord coming into His garden, and taking possession of it, receiving enjoyment from the fruitfulness of the church of Christ, His bride.

Then the second way in which we might read it, is as though the Lord says that He has, through His life on earth, gathered bitterness, which we know is the cross; He has experienced the sweetness of those whose mouths have dropped honey in their praises of Him; He has drunk the wine, — which is the joy of seeing souls turn to Him for salvation.

"I HAVE GATHERED MY MYRRH WITH MY SPICES."

You will remember we mentioned the bitterness in the lives of the Christians; not the root of bitterness which defiles, but the bitter experiences of life which are so hard for us to bear.

It is as though the Lord says to you, "I have come daughter, son, and bottled up all your tears."

The thing which has been bitterness, He will turn to sweetness and joy, if only we have patience to await His hour.

"I HAVE EATEN MY HONEY COMB WITH MY HONEY;"

He has received of us the praises we have offered to Him.

He has heard us when we spoke of Him. It has been as the sweetness of honey to the Lord.

"I HAVE DRUNK MY WINE WITH MY MILK:"
His joy has been full.

He has heard us as we gave forth the milk of the word. He has rejoiced to see us witness, to hear us preach the gospel in His name.

"EAT, O FRIENDS; DRINK, YEA, DRINK ABUNDANTLY, O, BELOVED."

Eat until you are full; drink until you are drunken is the full meaning. Drunk not with wine, but so filled with the Spirit of the Lord that you will be, as it were, overcome with the Spirit of God.

We have an abundant Lord. He is an abundant Giver. He giveth not the Spirit by measure. John 3:34. This attribute of the Lord is not only carried out in the things which are spiritual, but, praise to His dear name, He says, "I will divide Him a portion with the great." He is the giver of the double portion to all who, like Elisha, will humbly use it for God's glory.

vs. 2. "I SLEEP, BUT MY HEART WAKETH: IT IS THE
VOICE OF MY BELOVED THAT KNOCKETH,
SAYING, OPEN TO ME, MY SISTER, MY LOVE,
MY UNDEFILED: FOR MY HEAD IS FILLED
WITH DEW, AND MY LOCKS WITH THE DROPS
OF THE NIGHT."

"I SLEEP, BUT MY HEART WAKETH:"

In the following verses we have a picture of the church of Christ wanting the Lord to return but not altogether ready, and thereby, causing Him to delay His coming.

The bride is not altogether asleep. She is, as it were, only half-heartedly, "Waiting for the coming of the Lord Jesus Christ." 1 Cor. 1:7.

How true of many today who speak readily of the coming of the Lord. Often they even seem to want His return, but in their hearts and by their actions they hinder His return.

The Lord does not want His bride to only be half-awake but He wants us to be working and waiting. The half-asleep bride is in no state of readiness.

"IT IS THE VOICE OF MY BELOVED THAT KNOCKETH,
SAYING, OPEN TO ME, MY SISTER, MY LOVE, MY
UNDEFILED:"

The Lord is speaking in these days to the church through anointed prophecy, through visions, through the miraculous, as never before, trying to awaken her to realize that she is in the end time, that His coming is at hand, that He standeth at the door. Gently He calls to her, bidding her to be aroused to the urgency of the hour.

He loves her for she is clean and pure, washed in His precious blood, but she is so very indifferent, so careless in obeying His voice.

"FOR MY HEAD IS FILLED WITH DEW, AND MY LOCKS
WITH THE DROPS OF THE NIGHT."

He has already overstayed the time of His arrival. It has been a long night. All through the night the dew has been forming and the amount that has filled the head and locks of the Bridegroom show that it has been a longer night than average.

Morning is here; it is no time to continue to sleep. Bride of Christ awake!

vs. 3. "I HAVE PUT OFF MY COAT; HOW SHALL I PUT IT ON? I HAVE WASHED MY FEET; HOW SHALL I DEFILE THEM?"

"I HAVE PUT OFF MY COAT; HOW SHALL I PUT IT ON?"

A completely relaxed and unprepared bride! If she had been waiting for the Lord with a longing heart, she would not have put off her garments and retired. And now, it seems that she has laid aside the garment He gave her. She has been unappreciative of this garment which is of utter importance.

Now there is no time to put it on. We must wear it at all times. There is no time to change dresses when some one knocks at the door of your house. If you delay in opening the door by going to your room to dress up, it is quite likely your friend will be gone when you return. If you are expecting company, you will already have on the garment that you hoped to be wearing upon their arrival.

If the bride fully expects the return of her Lord, she would be in a state of absolute readiness.

"I HAVE WASHED MY FEET; HOW SHALL I DEFILE THEM."

The other day this was made so real to me. A Chinese woman staying in our home had bathed in the evening. Later she received company and when they left she escorted her friend down the road a short ways. When she returned I happened to see her washing her feet. So I said to her, "Didn't you have a bath already tonight, why then are you washing your feet again?" To which she replied, "I just walked outside and so they are dirty again."

I thought of this verse with its Eastern background. Here the bride had already washed her feet, so she was not expecting company to come, although her bridegroom had promised He would return to her soon. He expected her to be waiting and ready, or He would not have turned away in grief at her state of unpreparedness.

vs. 4. "MY BELOVED PUT HIS HAND BY THE HOLE OF THE DOOR, AND MY BOWELS WERE MOVED FOR HIM."

Now He gives her a special revelation of Himself to arouse her from her indifference.

I believe that in the last days the Lord will reveal Himself to the church in a special way to awaken her and prepare her for His return. Certainly we need it.

He shows her His hand. That is all. It is enough. I can't think of anything that would stir the church of Christ as much as His precious nail-pierced hands. When Thomas saw them, he fell on his face and cried, "My Lord, and my God." What had he asked to see? The face of Jesus? No. Even the angels of hell can come in the form of an angel of light. But only One bears the marks of the nail-prints in His hands.

When my life's work is ended
And I cross the swelling tide,
When the bright and glorious morning I shall see;
I shall know my redeemer when I reach the other shore
And His smile will be the first to welcome me

I shall know Him! I shall know Him!
As redeemed by His side I shall stand,
I shall know Him! I shall know Him!
By the prints of the nails in His hands.

Fanny J. Crosby

"MY BOWELS WERE MOVED FOR HIM."

None can stir the heart like Jesus! He is able to move our innermost being. The deepest recesses of a man's life are affected when he is revived by the Spirit of God.

As the Lord reveals Himself to His bride in these last days, He will stir and arouse and waken the deepest emotions that lie hidden in her.

vs. 5. "I ROSE UP TO OPEN TO MY BELOVED; AND MY HANDS DROPPED WITH MYRRH, AND MY FINGERS WITH SWEET SMELLING MYRRH, UPON THE HANDLES OF THE LOCK."

"I ROSE UP TO OPEN TO MY BELOVED:"

An awakened bride arises. The revelation which the Lord has given her of Himself has been enough to stir her to alertness. She is now ready to receive Him. No more does she worry about her garment, or her feet. She has only one desire, and that is for the Lord. We must open the door to fellowship with Him.

When will the church of Christ learn not to set her affections on things of this world? How easy it is to worship our beautiful churches and set our affections upon the building, rather than the Builder.

"Only seek material gain when that gain will mean a gain for my kingdom. Get away from money values altogether. Walk with me. Learn of me. Talk to me. Here lies your true happiness." Taken from "God Calling", a devotional diary.

"AND MY HANDS DROPPED WITH MYRRH, AND MY FINGERS WITH SWEET SMELLING MYRRH, UPON THE HANDLES OF THE LOCK."

The bride has arisen with a mighty anointing upon her. The revelation which the Lord gave her of Himself has not only stirred and revived the church, but has also brought a mighty anointing from the Lord Himself. Her hands have had the holy anointing oil poured upon them.

Hands are so important. They speak for themselves.

The hands of the Saviour tell the price He paid for our redemption, and the depths of the Love of God.

The hands of a baby speak of innocence and sweetness.

The hands of the little boy tell how he hates to wash.

The hands of the wayward and sinner are painted brown with the stain of sin's habits.

The hands of the beggar tremble for pity.

The hands of the addict are clutched in desperation.

The hands of the murderer are stained with blood.

The hands of the loving mother tell of years of toil for her family.

The hands of the blind are stretched out gropingly.

The hands of the Communists, clutched in a fist, speak of their zeal to gain others to their cause.

The hands of the woman with brilliant red nails tell of her love for elegance and fashion.

The hands of the hard working man never seem to be able to get washed altogether clean.

The hands of the betrothed and married speak of the vows their hearts have made.

The hands of the nurse minister aid and comfort to the sick.

The hands of the musician with their great ability of muscle control speak of years of patient practise and love of music.

The hands of the bride as she arises to bid her Lord come in, reveal the mighty anointing He has given to her.

All she needs to do, if she wants to know if He loves her, is to look at her hands. The anointing upon them speak a thousand words more powerful than any man could speak.

The miracle that has taken place upon her body, the body of Christ, the church, reminds us of the signs and wonders that He will do in these last days.

vs. 6. "I OPENED TO MY BELOVED; BUT MY BELOVED
HAD WITHDRAWN HIMSELF AND WAS GONE:
MY SOUL FAILED WHEN HE SPAKE: I SOUGHT
HIM, BUT I COULD NOT FIND HIM; I CALLED
HIM, BUT HE GAVE ME NO ANSWER."

She was not ready for His coming, so He withdraws Himself and leaves her, but not without having first given her the precious anointing of oil.

A time of testing is given to her. After the great anointing, He allows her to go through the greatest test of her entire life.

The time of fiery persecution which awaits the church of God will not be met with and conquered by a powerless church, but one that will be anointed as never before in its entire history. Even a greater anointing than she had at her beginning will come upon her in the last days.

She confesses she had first of all failed Him when He spoke, but now, how she longs for His return.

The soul that goes through persecution is very much unattached to the world. Nothing ever will loosen the church of Christ from the desire and love of the world as much as persecution. Because she was not ready without the persecution, He finds it necessary to allow her to suffer so that she will truly be prepared for Him.

vs. 7. "THE WATCHMEN THAT WENT ABOUT THE
CITY FOUND ME, THEY SMOTE ME, THEY
WOUNDED ME; THE KEEPERS OF THE WALLS
TOOK AWAY MY VEIL FROM ME."

Here we see these backslidden, unregenerated watchmen once again. The first time she met them in 3:3 they did not help her to find the Lord, but they at least did not persecute her. Now it seems as though an evil spirit of hell has come upon them, and they are filled with a desire to persecute the lovely bride who seeks so earnestly for her Lord and Master's return.

We will no doubt be amazed that it is the watchmen who are supposed to be in charge of Zion who are the worst offenders against the anointed bride.

Why should their fury be so great now? Because they see her hands. The sign of the anointing of God upon the church, the earnestness and desperation in which she cries out this time as she did not do the last time, makes them angry.

They smite her, they wound her, but they can never quench the power of God in her life.

All the persecution of hell will not be able to rob the anointed bride of Christ in the last days.

"THEY TOOK AWAY MY VEIL."

The most embarrassing thing they could do was to tear away her modest covering and gaze upon her in mocking laughter.

Many of the "keepers of the walls" will be used by the Evil One to bring embarrassment upon the bride of Christ. They will call her up before councils as they did Peter and John of old. They will cruelly examine her and question her, not because they want to learn the truth, but because their hearts are filled with an evil desire to bring shame and embarrassment upon her.

Yes, there will be a price to pay for the anointing which will fall upon the bride in the last days.

Will you, will I, be able to suffer the embarrassment of being smitten, wounded and mocked to shame?

Will we be able to drink the cup that our Saviour drank for us?

vs. 8. "I CHARGE YOU, O DAUGHTERS OF JERUSALEM, IF YE FIND MY BELOVED, THAT YE TELL HIM, THAT I AM SICK OF LOVE."

Most of the times that the bride speaks to the "Daughters of Jerusalem she delivers a charge, a command to them.

Always she seems to be afraid that they will rob her of her communion and fellowship with the Lord.

Still she holds authority over them because of her intimate relationship with the Lord. She demands that a message be given to the Lord.

"I AM SICK OF LOVE."

Once again, in great earnestness she repeats the words of 2:5.

The first time she spoke these words of her love to Him in private. Now she confesses it before others.

What are some of the symptoms of love-sickness?
Loss of appetite.
Inability to sleep.
Loss of all other interests in life.
Desire only for the companionship of the loved one.
The love-sick person knows no shame or pride.
Their one thought at all times is of the one they love.

Test your love for the Lord by these symptoms.

— Do you love Him enough that it is easy to fast?
— Do you often not sleep for thinking of the Lord, and upon your bed you spend sleepless hours filled with praises to Him?
— Is your first desire the kingdom of God?
— Do you desire His companionship more than that of others, and find yourself talking to Him often?
— Are you ever ashamed of Him at any time or ever too proud to speak of Him to others?
— Are you always thinking about Him?

How wonderful if you can say yes to all this. Then truly you have fallen in love with Jesus.

vs. 9. "WHAT IS THY B E L O V E D M O R E T H A N
A N O T H E R B E L O V E D, O THOU FAIREST
AMONG WOMEN? WHAT IS THY BELOVED
M O R E T H A N ANOTHER BELOVED, THAT
THOU DOST SO CHARGE US?"

It is easy to see they don't love Him like she does. They
can't see why she should love Him so dearly.

They see her as the fairest among women, and recognise
her as one that is set apart, fairer than all others. This is the
second time she is called "the fairest among women."

The interest of the Daughters of Jerusalem is at last aroused;
they want to know more about Him. They are beginning to
get interested.

The witness of the bride of Christ in these days to the
daughters of Jerusalem, the Jews, is growing every year. The
Jews are beginning to wonder more and more about Jesus Christ.
Many are starting to ask about Him. Many are reading the New
Testament.

Some scholars think 1:8 was spoken by the daughters of
Jerusalem, if that is so, then you will notice that they helped
her find Him the first time. Remember it was the Jews who
brought the message of salvation to the Gentiles. God used Paul,
Peter, and other men who were Jews. In fact nearly all of the
early church were Jews. The Spirit of God when outpoured at
Pentecost, was likely outpoured upon 120 Jews. However, the
nation as a whole rejected Him and were indifferent, but now
they are inquiring.

An anointed bride with the anointing oil upon her has
stirred them. When the Jews see the miraculous again, and the
wonders wrought in the name of Jesus, they will wonder, "What
is thy beloved, more than another beloved?"

The following Poem given to a child of God in the hours
of the night shows the urgency of the times.

"A MESSAGE TO THE JEWS"

Tonight I was awakened
With a message for the Jew
God layed a burden on my heart.
He said to write it, too.

Oh, hasten warn my people
Before it is too late
And tell them I am coming soon
I will not hestitate.

Oh, yes I'm coming quickly
In the twinkling of an eye
To catch my blood washed throng away
To meet me in the sky.

I came two thousand years ago
And died upon the cross.
They would not own me as their King,
Go tell them they are lost.

This time I'll come in judgment
On all who from me turn
My wrath I'll pour upon them
Because my love they've spurned.

But tell them I still love them
And want to save them now
For I am their Messiah
And to me they must bow.

For in my book 'tis written
That every knee shall bend
And every tongue shall speak of me
As Christ, the Saviour then.

Mrs. V. Tate

vs. 10. "MY BELOVED IS WHITE AND RUDDY, THE
CHIEFEST AMONG TEN THOUSAND."

"MY BELOVED IS WHITE AND RUDDY."

The Hebrew word "tsach" means bright, shining clearness.

The whiteness she refers to is not paleness of flesh but the glorious brightness and radiance that Daniel saw when he said, "As the appearance of lightening."   Dan. 10:6.

Peter and James and John saw the same when they later reported that his raiment was white and glistening.   Luke. 9:29.

John the beloved saw Him whose countenance was as the sun that shineth in his strength.   Rev. 1:16.

RUDDY has been translated from "adhom" which means dark red.   It could betoken health and ruddiness, but I believe it should be linked with Rev. 19:13, "And He was clothed with a vesture dipped in blood: and His name is called "The Word of God."   John saw Jesus as the. Great Judge, even as Isaiah had seen Him.   Isa. 63:2-4.

"THE CHIEFEST AMONG TEN THOUSAND."

The Hebrew of the American revised Version renders it, "Marked out by a Banner."

We all know the banner or ensign that marked out our Lord and made Him the chiefest of ten thousand to our soul. Read again 2:4.   Remember what we said.   It was the old rugged cross.

There is none like our Lord.

> "Dearer than all, Yes, dearer than all,
> He is my King, Before Him I fall,
> No one like Jesus, My soul can enthral,
> Jesus is dearer; Far dearer than all."

This was one of the choruses that the young people of our camp sang the summer that I was saved.   How dear and precious He was!   How wonderful the joy of new found faith!   Every time I hear that chorus, or sing it myself, it takes me back to that little camp ground in Ontario, and again I see the joy of the faces around me and the dear friends who had prayed so earnestly for my soul's salvation.   It was a new experience for me, a complete change of heart, to find that suddenly, after so many years of rebellion against the Lord, that He was now dearer than all to me.

vs. 11. "HIS HEAD IS AS THE MOST FINE GOLD, HIS LOCKS ARE BUSHY, AND BLACK AS A RAVEN."

You will remember that when Nebuchadnezzar had the dream in which he saw the image of a great man whose head was of gold, that God gave the interpretation of it to Daniel. He told him in Dan. 2:37 that the head of gold was the king himself. He said, "Thou, O king, art a king of kings: for the God of heaven hath given thee a kingdom, power and strength and glory."

The description of the Bridegroom which we are about to study in the following verse begins with this beautiful statement that his head is as the most fine gold.

This is because he is, not as Nebuchadnezzar was, A king of kings, but The King of Kings! Truly God has given Him the Kingdom — and of His kingdom there shall be no end. Luke 1:33.

The power — "The head of all principalities and power" Col. 2:10.

The strength — which He showed with His arm. Luke 1:51.

The glory — which He entered into through His suffering. Luke 24:26.

In Rev. 5:12 we have the final and complete picture of Christ as He enters into His rights. "Saying with a loud voice, Worthy is the Lamb which was slain to receive Power, and Riches and Wisdom, and Strength and Honour and Glory and Blessing."

How much more did He receive than Nebuchadnezzar! How much greater He is! Truly He is the King of Kings and the Lord of Lords. He is all fine gold as the bride has said.

"HIS LOCKS ARE BUSHY AND BLACK AS A RAVEN."

The significance of these words is most startling. Under the divine inspiration the author of the Song of Songs who has in a few words so gloriously pictured the deity of Christ, in the same sentence tells of His humanity.

The contrast of the raven black hair and the fine gold is most unique.

He was truly all God. He was truly all man.

— He was conceived by the Holy Spirit, yet He had a human birth.

— He confounded His teachers at the age of 12, yet His development was human.

— He carried the names, Wonderful, Councellor, the Prince of Peace, the Everlasting Father, yet He carried the human name of Joshua (Jesus).

— He rose from the dead triumphant, yet He had to be awakened by the disciples when a storm arose at sea.

In His Deity and in His humanity He was most perfect, most unique, and most wonderful.

The marks of His humanity He will always carry with Him in the nailprints of His hands, and feet, the stripes on His back and the wound in His side.

Every time we look at Him in glory we will see, as it were, the deity of His Golden Head and the humanity of His Raven locks.

He entered into His power through that which He suffered in His humanity.

vs. 12. "HIS EYES ARE THE EYES OF DOVES BY THE RIVERS OF WATERS, WASHED WITH MILK, AND FITLY SET."

"HIS EYES ARE THE EYES OF DOVES."

This verse reveals to us the fullness of the Holy Spirit which filled Christ.

His eyes speak of His Spiritual insight. Truly He has spiritual discernment in every thing that concerns His children. When He looks at you He doesn't see the house you live in only, but the person that you are inside. He sees your heart's deepest longings, your soul's greatest need.

"BY THE RIVERS OF WATERS."

The Rivers of water also speak of the blessed Holy Spirit's greatest fullness.

With absolute authority He spoke these words, "If any man thirst, let him come unto me and drink." John 7:37.

"WASHED WITH MILK AND FITLY SET."

The Hebrew of the words "fitly set" is "sitting in fulness." That is, His spiritual power and insight were given to Him in complete fullness.

— "It pleased the Father that in Him should all fulness dwell." Col. 1:19.
— "For in Him dwelleth all the fulness of the Godhead bodily." Col. 2:9.

The Words which He spoke were words anointed with the power of the Holy Spirit. He spoke the Word of God because He was the Word of God.

"For He Whom God hath sent speaketh the words of God; for God giveth not the Spirit by measure unto Him." John 3:34.

vs. 13.   "HIS CHEEKS ARE AS A BED OF SPICES, AS SWEET FLOWERS: HIS LIPS LIKE LILIES, DROPPING SWEET SMELLING MYRRH."

"HIS CHEEKS ARE AS A BED OF SPICES."

What was there about the cheeks or face of the Lord that showed forth to the world the fragrance of the sweetest spices, the pleasantest flowers?

In His teaching, Christ said, "And unto him that smiteth thee on the one cheek offer also the other." Luke 6:29.

Jesus not only taught meekness, but He lived what He taught.

What did He do when they struck Him on the face? Luke 22:64. He answered not a word.

What did He do when they spit on His face? Matt. 27:30, 26:67. He answered not a word.

What did He do when the blood ran down His cheeks from the wounds on his brow that were made by the crown of thorns? He answered not a word.

Isaiah under the inspiration of the Holy Spirit, when picturing the crucified Lord in His hour of suffering said, "He hath no form nor comeliness: and when we shall see Him, there is no beauty that we should desire Him." 53:2b.

Yes, it would have been impossible to see with the natural eye any beauty in the bloody, bruised, painful face of our Lord, as the spittle of the blasphemer lay dried on His cheeks —

Yet, the author of S. of S. saw in all His suffering the fragrance of the sweet and gentle Spirit of the Lord revealed through His shameful suffering.

"HIS LIPS LIKE LILIES, DROPPING SWEET SMELLING MYRRH."

The Lips of our Lord spoke the purest of words. Lilies are the flowers of purity. The Words of Life which Jesus spoke were, like the lilies, undefiled. What anointing and what power came forth from His mouth! No matter to whom He spoke, His words were the words of God.

To the cruel accusers of the woman caught in adultry; —

"He that is without sin among you, let him first cast a stone at her." John 8:7.

To the sinful woman that longed for forgiveness; —

"Neither do I condemn thee: go, and sin no more."

At the beginning of His ministry to the people of His town; —

"The Spirit of the Lord is upon me, because He hath anointed me to preach the gospel to the poor; He hath sent me to heal the broken hearted, to preach deliverance to the captives, and recovering of sight to the blind, to set at liberty them that are bruised, To preach the acceptable year of the Lord." Luke 4:18-20.

To the future early church leaders —

"Follow me, and I will make you fishers of men." Matt. 4:19.

To the ruler that came to Him by night —

"Ye must be born again." John 3:7.

To those who would trick Him, that they might accuse Him —

"Render unto Caesar the things which are Caesar's and unto God the things which are God's." Matt. 22:21.

To those who crucified Him —

"Father forgive them, for they know not what they do." Luke 23:34.

To Mary who came seeking Him —

"Woman, why weepest thou?" John 20:13.

We could go on and on. But we know that always it would be the same. Everything He said was pure and anointed.

vs. 14. "HIS HANDS ARE AS GOLD RINGS SET WITH THE BERYL: HIS BELLY IS AS BRIGHT IVORY OVERLAID WITH SAPPHIRES."

We saw His deity in His head. Now we see it in His hands.

With His hands He made the world. They are the hands of God.

Beryl speaks of judgement. In His hands are the marks of judgment.

"HIS BELLY, (His body) IS AS FINE IVORY."

Ivory is a hard, creamy-white substance derived from the tusks of elephants and other animals.

There are several different kinds. Live ivory which is scarce and dead ivory which is plentiful but inferior. This dead ivory comes from Siberia where large animals called mammoths and mastodons once lived. Today their tusks are dug from the frozen ground where they have been preserved for thousand of years.

Elephant ivory from Africa is the best quality.

Poorer quality ivory comes from the tusks, horns and teeth of the hippopotamus, walrus, and narwhal.

Imitation ivory is produced from the nut of the ivory palm, as well as from celluloid and certain other plastics.

Why do we mention all this? Simply to make us realize that the ivory which is mentioned in this verse is of the very best and highest quality. It says, "Fine ivory". In Him is Life. The Live ivory is what is referred to by the anointed writer. He is the Resurrection and the Life.

Another thing about ivory is that it will bend without breaking.

How wonderfully significant then are these words, "A bone of Him shall not be broken."

Now, we know that it is also spoken that we are the body of Christ — "For His body's sake, which is the church." Col. 1:24. All through the centuries He has been preparing "His body" and forming it into a thing of beauty and quality.

"OVERLAID WITH SAPPHIRES."

The sapphire is a beautiful, transparent gem. Sapphires of all colors of the rainbow are found. The blue sapphires are the most valuable. Large ones are equal to a fine diamond in value.

Isaiah caught a glimpse of the "body of Christ" as he penned the words in Isa. 54:11, "I will lay thy foundations with sapphires." The glory and beauty of Christ shines forth today through His body, the church.

vs. 15. "HIS LEGS ARE AS PILLARS OF MARBLE, SET UPON SOCKETS OF FINE GOLD: HIS COUNTENANCE IS AS LEBANON, EXCELLENT AS THE CEDARS."

"HIS LEGS ARE AS PILLARS OF MARBLE."

Ancient people made their finest buildings of either granite or marble, just as men do today.

Marble is any limestone that is hard enough to take a polish. Whereas ordinary limestone is made up of fragments of shells or irregular grains of calcium carbonate. Marble which comes out of limestone has been changed by metamorphosis which has made it more uniform in hardness and grain throughout so that it can be carved better than ordinary limestone. It also takes a higher polish because it is freed from small cavities and pores. (Metamorphosis is a word used by biologists to describe the rather abrupt changes of transformations which occur in the life of such living creatures as the frog, the butterfly or moth). Marble then is limestone that is transformed into a substance much superior than it originally was. The finest marble is white.

Even as the butterfly comes forth transformed from the cocoon, and the marble after lying hidden for centuries is transformed from ordinary limestone into a thing of beauty, so our Lord came forth from the grave in greater glory than He had before His death. He knew that this greater glory awaited him after death when He said, "Now is the Son of man glorified, and God is glorified in Him." John 13:32.

Legs are the limbs that support the body. Pillars are columns that support a building. Legs then are the pillars of the body. The body of Christ, the church, then is supported by pillars, columns of the finest of marble, marble which is spiritual and not material, marble which has been transformed by the death and resurrection of the Lord into that which is perfect, without flaw and "able to take the highest polish."

Marble lasts a long time. The Parthenon of Athens, through which Paul walked in his day, still would stand upon its pillars of marble if man had not destroyed it in wars. Much of it is still there. The church of Christ stands eternal because it has a sure foundation in the pillars of Christ

> — Pillars of the finest of marble,
> — Pillars of resurrection life.

"SET UPON SOCKETS OF FINE GOLD."

The image which Nebuchadnezzar saw in his dream began with a head of gold, but ended with feet of clay.

The feet of our Lord, these sockets of fine gold, are not so. His entire image is one of perfection. It is crowned in deity; it is grounded in deity. From head to toe the picture is perfect.

"HIS COUNTENANCE IS AS LEBANON, EXCELLENT AS THE CEDARS."

The evergreen trees growing upon the ever white mountainside of Lebanon's higher elevation are a picture of the never-changing nature of our Lord.

"I am the Lord, I change not." Mal. 3:6.

"Jesus Christ, the same, yesterday, and today and forever." Heb. 13:8.

"But Thou art the same, and Thy years shall not fail." Heb. 1:12b.

vs. 16. "HIS MOUTH IS MOST SWEET: YEA, HE IS ALTOGETHER LOVELY. THIS IS MY BELOVED, AND THIS IS MY FRIEND, O DAUGHTERS OF JERUSALEM.

"HIS MOUTH IS MOST SWEET."

The description is now ending by a repeated reference once again to the words of His mouth. Words of sweetness.

"YEA, HE IS ALTOGETHER LOVELY."

Our wonderful Lord. Our wonderful Lord.
By angels and seraphs in heaven adored.

The fairest of ten thousand.

Lest she should have forgotten to mention some of His virtues, the bride in closing says, "He is altogether lovely.

"THIS IS MY BELOVED, AND THIS IS MY FRIEND."

His love is complete — the love of a Lover, the love of a Friend, the love of a Father, the love of a Brother. (Does not He often call her, My sister?) 5:1.

I would like to quote from the reading for May 14, of Devotional Diary, "God Calling."

"Yield in all things to My tender insistence, but remember that I yield, too, to yours. Ask not only the big things I have told you, but ask the little tender signs of Love. Remember that I came as the world's Great Lover. Never think of My Love as only a tender compassion and forgiveness. It is that, but it is also the Love of a Lover who shows His Love by countless words and actions and by tender thoughts.

What man calls conversion is often only the discovery of a Great Friend.
What man calls religion is the knowledge of the Great Friend."
What man calls holiness is the imitation of the Great Friend."

Yes, we can say with the bride. "He is My Beloved, and He is my Friend."

"O DAUGHTERS OF JERUSALEM."

And so she ends her beautiful description of Him Who is the Bridegroom to her and the Messiah to the daughters of Jerusalem.

CHAPTER SIX

vs. 1. "WHITHER IS THY BELOVED GONE, O THOU FAIREST AMONG WOMEN? WHITHER IS THY BELOVED TURNED ASIDE? THAT WE MAY SEEK HIM WITH THEE."

In verse 5:9 they (the Daughters of Jerusalem) the Jews were wondering and beginning to inquire about the bride's beloved. They had asked her, "What is thy beloved more than another beloved?"

She has just finished giving them the glorious testimony of all that Jesus means to her. She has told them of —

His deity — verse 11
His humanity — verse 11
His mighty anointing with Spiritual power. vs. 12
His humility and submission to suffering. vs. 13
His words of power, the Word of Life. vs. 13
The judgment He bore in His hands. vs. 14
The resurrection life which dwells in His body. vs. 14
The eternal Christ as the pillars of the church,
    (His body). vs. 15
The foundation of deity. vs. 15
His immutability. vs. 15
The sweetness of His words. vs. 16
The friend He is to her. vs. 16

Truly this has been a complete revelation of the Lord Jesus Christ. After He has been revealed to the Jews, they begin to seek Him, together with the bride.

How can we hasten the return of our Lord? — not only by preparing our own hearts, but by giving a faithful witness to the Daughters of Jerusalem. As they begin to turn from their rejection of the Lord Jesus as the Messiah, and begin to seek Him too, then, all things are ready for His return.

vs. 2. "MY BELOVED IS GONE DOWN INTO HIS GAR-
DEN, TO THE BEDS OF SPICES, TO FEED IN
THE GARDENS, AND TO GATHER LILIES."

"MY BELOVED IS GONE DOWN INTO HIS GARDEN."

The communion of the bride and her Beloved is restored.
She knows where He is. Who has told her? How does she
know? Remember that she is the garden. She knows who
enters through her gates. She knows that He has come back in,
in answer to her crying need.

When did He come in? — when she was witnessing to the
daughters of Jerusalem.

The first time He had left her she brought Him back by
clinging fast to Him. 3:4. Now she has a new power with
Him by Her faithful witness to the Daughters of Jerusalem.
While she is telling them all about Him, He silently returns to
her garden.

"TO THE BEDS OF SPICES, TO FEED IN THE GARDENS,
AND TO GATHER LILIES."

A completed reunion. Companionship and Fellowship is all
restored.

He has come to gather His lilies. What are His lilies?
In 2:2 we read that we are His lilies.

How beautifully is the doctrine of the rapture pictured in
this verse.

Gathering the lilies! Yes, we are living in that hour now.
While the church as never before, is witnessing to the Jews and
a new burden is coming upon many hearts for the Daughters
of Jerusalem, the Lord is about to come into His garden and
gather His lilies.

He will pick us out from among the thorns that have caused
us great suffering and miseries; we shall be plucked up by His
nail-pierced hands and gathered into His loving arms to be placed
on show in His mansions above, for all eternity.

vs. 3. "I AM MY BELOVED'S, AND MY BELOVED IS
MINE: HE FEEDETH AMONG THE LILIES."

This verse is the same as in 2:16.

She fully belongs to Him. No one else has any claims
on her.

vs. 4. "THOU ART BEAUTIFUL, O M Y L O V E , A S
TIRZAH, COMELY AS JERUSALEM, TERRIBLE
AS AN ARMY WITH BANNERS."

"THOU ART BEAUTIFUL, O MY LOVE, AS TIRZAH."

Tirzah means "delight", which describes its beauty. It was
at one time an ancient Canaanite city which was conquered by
the children of Israel. Joshua 12:24. Later Jeroboam, the first
king of Israel, after the kingdom was divided, lived in it; thus
it became a royal city. Tirzah was situated in a lofty and
delightful location surrounded by olive groves.

It seems strange that Solomon should mention this city,
which, after his death, under his son's rule, would become the
rival city of Jerusalem. In the hearts of all of Israel no city was
as dear as Jerusalem, but later, when the nation was divided, they
set their affections upon Tirzah. Solomon did not know the
future. He had no way of knowing that this city was to play
such a great role in the years in which his son would lose most
of his kingdom. So we see how divinely inspired were these
words. For the Lord knew the future. He knew how the
hearts of men would change. He knew that it was to become
the royal city of the ten tribes.

"COMELY AS JERUSALEM."

Jerusalem, habitation of peace, the city surrounded by hills.
It also is remarkably high, situated on the edge of one of the
highest table-lands of the country.

It was important to the Israelites not only because it was the royal city of their king, before the dividing of the kingdom, but because it was the city of the Great King. Psalm 48:2. The prophets had always prophesied that some day the Messiah would set up His kingdom in this city.

Jeremiah, in Lam. 2:15 gives us a good idea of the opinion of all the world as regards to this city. "Is this the city that men call the perfection of beauty, the joy of the whole earth?"

Are we then, the bride of Christ, not given the highest of honours when we realize that the Lord has said that we are as beautiful as the delightful Tirzah, as comely as the perfect beauty of Jerusalem, the joy of the whole earth?

"TERRIBLE AS AN ARMY WITH BANNERS."

The more easily understood translation, "Awe-inspiring as bannered hosts" is more correct.

How well we remember in the last world war, when the soldiers paraded through the cities of our land to the music of the military bands, how it used to inspire awe in our hearts as we looked upon the faces of those who marched forward with such courage into terrible and bloody battles.

When our oldest boy, David, was 3 years old, he had the opportunity of seeing a large military parade in Niagara Falls, N.Y. Hundreds of soldiers came marching across the great Rainbow bridge from Niagara Falls, Canada. The sight of these marching men and women in their uniforms, carrying their banners, and the music of the bands had such an affect upon little David that he began to shake and tremble and soon he was crying and hanging on to my father and myself.

Truly the awe-struck little boy is a good picture of the affect that the bride of Christ should have upon the world today. When will the bride stir in the hearts of the ungodly and indifferent such reverent dread, inspired by deity, and solemn wonder as she should? Surely we must lack something of the power to inspire men or we would have been a greater affect upon the world. Could it be because of the fact that our ranks are divided?

When the world stands on the side-lines and watches the church militant marching as to war with the cross of Jesus going on before, does it see a church and army that is more at war with each other than against the devil?

God help us to be one.

It won't be until the Lord's prayer is answered, "That they may be one, even as We are" that the church will be, as the bridegroom of Song of Songs says, "Awe-inspiring as an army with banners."

vs. 5. "TURN AWAY THINE EYES FROM ME, FOR THEY HAVE OVERCOME ME: THY HAIR IS AS A FLOCK OF GOATS THAT APPEAR FROM GILEAD."

In verse 4:9 we read that with only one of her eyes, the bride had stolen the heart of the Beloved Bridegroom. Now, as she has come marching home in all her glory, it is as though she gazes upon the Lord her Saviour with both of her eyes.

As He looks upon His bride, the sight is so wonderful that He can hardly bear it. With what great joy He shall gather us home to present us faultless before the presence of His glory with exceeding joy. Jude 1:24.

In the column of one Bible I read, "For they have puffed me up," in place of, "For they have overcome me:"

With great pride Jesus will present the bride to the hosts of heaven in His Father's house.

"THY HAIR IS AS A FLOCK OF GOATS THAT APPEAR FROM GILEAD."

Again He mentions her power and the secret of its source, as in 4:1.

vs. 6,7. "THY TEETH ARE AS A FLOCK OF SHEEP WHICH GO UP FROM THE WASHING, WHEREOF EVERY ONE BEARETH TWINS, AND THERE IS NOT ONE BARREN AMONG THEM."

"AS A PIECE OF POMEGRANATE ARE THY TEMPLES WITH THY LOCKS."

A repetition of 4:2 and 4:3b. He reviews again the

1. Joy of the bride shown by her lovely smile.
2. Purity and peace of mind which is here. "Thou wilt keep Him in perfect peace whose mind is stayed on Thee, because he trusteth in Thee." Isa. 26:3.

vs. 8. "THERE ARE THREESCORE QUEENS, AND FOURSCORE CONCUBINES, AND VIRGINS WITHOUT NUMBER."

You will remember that in 3:7 we referred to the 60 queens of the palace. Each of them having a high place of authority; each with a special gaurdian angel to protect her.

Now again it mentions these 60 queens. Also, it mentions the 80 concubines (small wives) and then the large number of virgins that had been selected throughout the land by the officers of the king and brought into the harem to be prepared for the King's final acceptance.

All of them, the virgins, concubines, queens and the chosen bride were members of the royal household. I can't see how these, who are members of the royal household can possibly refer to the unsaved, and non-Christian as some commentators seem to think.

All through the Bible we see the same picture. In the ministry of Christ on earth, there were

1. The multitude who followed.
2. The 500 who were faithful to the ascension.

3. The 120 who persevered to the upper room.
4. The 12 who were the specially chosen disciples.
5. The 3 who knew His deeper secrets and went with Him to places that others were not invited to go.

In the Book of Revelation, that wonderful vision which the Lord gave John on the Isle of Patmos, we also see the same thing. We read in Revelation about —

1. The Great multitude which no man could number. 7:9
2. The 144000. 7:4
3. The Bride of Christ. 19:7
4. The twenty-four elders. 5:8, 14
5. Twelve thrones seating the judges. Rev. 20:4, Matt. 19:28
6. The 4 living creatures. 5:8, 14
7. Finally, both small and great. 19:5

Who are the 24 elders? The Bible does not tell us. Nor do we know who the 4 living creatures are which are seated in such high positions of honour next to the throne of God.

But God knows who they are, and He knows to whom to give these places of honour. He also knows just who will be included in each of the above mentioned groups.

He did say, "To him that overcometh will I grant to sit with me in my throne." Rev. 3:21.

To the mother of John and James, however, he could not promise that her sons would have the seats on His left and right side. He told them that it shall be given them for whom it is prepared of my Father.

Certainly there will be a distinction. Dan. 12:3 says, "They that be wise shall shine as the brightness of the firmament: and they that turn many to righteousness, as the stars for over and ever."

vs. 9. "MY DOVE, MY UNDEFILED IS BUT ONE; SHE IS THE ONLY ONE OF HER MOTHER, SHE IS THE CHOICE ONE OF HER THAT BARE HER. THE DAUGHTERS SAW HER, AND BLESSED HER; YEA, THE QUEENS AND THE CONCUBINES, AND THEY PRAISED HER.

"MY DOVE, MY UNDEFILED IS BUT ONE."

If you will notice closely in your Bible, the adverb "but" has been inserted by the translators. This almost seems to change the meaning. If we leave it out it makes us understand more clearly that the bride is not just one individual, but a group of people who are at oneness with each other in the Lord.

"SHE IS THE ONLY ONE OF HER MOTHER: SHE IS THE CHOICE ONE OF HER THAT BARE HER."

"Choice" or "Pure" as in the American Revised Version.

In this sentence two words were added by the translators, changing it from, "She is the one of her mother, she is the choice of her that bare her."

We know from 1:6 that she was not the only child her mother had. Therefore the real meaning of this verse is not that she was the only child of the family, but that she was "The" child, the chosen one. She was, as David, anointed from her youth and set apart for the place she would fill in the kingdom of God.

"THE DAUGHTERS SAW HER, AND BLESSED HER, YEA, THE QUEENS AND THE CONCUBINES, AND THEY PRAISED HER."

Not only was she marked out by her anointing to the members of her family, but, after entering the royal household, she still is called out from among the others.

The Bridegroom, as it were, looked down upon His Royal household and without any difficulty whatsoever, He selected the bride. She was marked out for Him by her special love for Him and by her purity. In Revelation we read that she was without fault before the throne of God.

Her purity and spotlessness causes the others in the royal household to praise her and bless her.

In his vision and revelation of heaven and things to come, John not only saw the bride, but he saw many other companies of people, both small and great.   19:5.

vs. 10.   "WHO IS SHE THAT LOOKETH FORTH AS THE MORNING, FAIR AS THE MOON, CLEAR AS THE SUN, AND TERRIBLE AS AN ARMY WITH BANNERS?"

"WHO IS SHE THAT LOOKETH FORTH AS THE MORNING."

She is as the morning breaking across the horizon, fair and glorious, tinting the sky in pink and rosy hues, turning the blackness of the night into hope of a new day.

Yes, the rapture of the bride will usher in a new day for her, a day of gladness, eternal.

"FAIR AS THE MOON."

How lovely the moon looks on a clear night. It shines as a lamp in a dark sky, lighting up the world.

As the moon light is the reflection of the sun, so the bride of Christ on earth is a reflection of the Light of the Son of God.

"CLEAR AS THE SUN."

Gradually her brightness grows greater, until when she shall see Him, a great change shall take place in her; she shall shine in greater glory and brightness.

"Beloved, now are we the sons of God, and it doth not yet appear what we shall be; but we know that, when He shall appear, we shall be like Him; for we shall see Him as He is." 1 John 3:2.

"TERRIBLE AS AN ARMY WITH BANNERS."

The triumphant bride is as the victorious army. As the fair moon shineth in the darkness of the night, she shall go forth in a day of darkness and gloominess, a day of clouds and thickness. Isa. 60:1, 2.

Isa. 60:1, 2. "Arise, shine, for thy light is come, for the glory of the Lord is risen upon thee. For, behold, darkness shall cover the earth, and gross darkness the people; but the Lord shall arise upon thee, and His glory shall be seen upon thee."

A great people and a strong; there hath not been ever the like. The morning spread upon the mountains will be her signal to go forth. Joel 2:2.

What a wonderful prophectic revelation Joel had of this "terrible army with banners."

"There hath not been ever the like, neither shall be any more after it, even to the years of generations and generations."

"A fire devoureth before them, and behind them a flame burneth;"

"The appearance of them is as the appearance of horses: as horsemen, so shall they run."

"Like the noise of chariots on the tops of the mountain shall they leap, like the noise of a flame of fire that devoureth the stubble, as a strong people set in battle array."

"Before their face the people shall be much pained: all faces shall gather blackness."

"They shall run like mighty men; they shall climb the wall like men of war; and they shall march every one on his ways, and they shall not break their ranks:"

"Neither shall one thrust another; they shall walk every one in his path: and when they fall upon the sword, they shall not be wounded."

"The Lord shall utter His voice before His army; for His camp is very great: for He is strong that executeth His word: for the day of the Lord is great and very terrible and who shall abide?"

Several things about this army stand out and bear repeating.

1. The fire of God goes before it and follows behind. Without this fire of God this army would be unarmed.

2. The oneness and unity is so beautiful to see.
     "They shall march every one in his ways."
     "They shall not break their ranks."
     "Neither shall one thrust another."

vs. 11. "I WENT DOWN INTO THE GARDEN OF NUTS TO SEE THE FRUITS OF THE VALLEY, AND TO SEE WHETHER THE VINE FLOURISHED, AND THE POMEGRANTES BUDDED."

The bride is searching through her garden. She knows that time is short, and she is making sure that it is fruitful and healthy and flourishing as it should.

I believe that the "last day revival" will be a day in which we will search our hearts as never before. It will be a day of sifting, a day of self-judgment. God help up to judge ourselves and lay aside now the sins that would hinder us from being in the victorious army, the bride of Christ.

How about your garden? How is your communion with Christ? Is the vine flourishing, or has it dried up?

Have the pomegranates budded? Pomegranates are the fruit of righteousness. Remember we are made clean by the Blood of Christ, but we must not forget that the bride of Christ made herself ready by her righteous acts. Rev. 19:7, 8.

vs. 12. "OR EVER I WAS AWARE, MY SOUL MADE ME LIKE THE CHARIOTS OF AMMINADIB."

The R.V. has translated, "set me among" for "made me like."

Amminadib is probably another form of Amminadab which means "one of the prince's people."

The bride is speaking. She is saying, "Before I was aware my soul set me among the chariots that belong to the people of the Prince."

We all remember when Elijah was lifted into heaven, that there appeared a chariot of fire and horses of fire. Elisha, when he saw it cried, "My father, my father, the chariot of Israel, and the horsemen thereof." 11 Kings 2:12.

Later when Elisha was sick and on his death bed, the king of Israel, Joash, came down to see him and stood by his bed weeping. The Lord gave the king a revelation of the passing of the soul of Elisha. Strangly enough, that although Elijah went to heaven without tasting of death, and Elisha went by way of the death bed, in both cases they were carried away by the same chariot of fire and horsemen of fire. At the death-bed of Elisha, the king either had this revealed to him by the Holy Spirit or by a vision. King Joash, upon realizing that Elisha was soon to leave this world and go to heaven, and seeing the way in which his soul would go, cried, "O my father, my father, the chariot of Israel, and the horsemen thereof." 11 Kings 13:14.

Both of these Old Testament prophets and saints were given the same honourable reception into heaven. Their souls were received up and accompanied with the chariot of Israel.

The Israelites had their own special guardian angel. In Dan. 12:1 we read that Michael is the great prince that standeth for the Israelites.

Whether the prince referred to is Michael or the Lord Jesus Himself, it does not say. We know though, that it is the chariot that accompanied Elijah and Elisha which now so suddenly, before the bride is aware of it, has come upon her as she is in the garden, and she is "set among it."

We can be sure that the bride of Christ is made up of saints who have already died as well as those who will be taken up in the rapture at the coming of the Lord.

Elijah and Elisha are an example of this.   Although Elisha died, still he was carried away into heaven with the same glory as Elijah who did not taste death.   These two men are a type of the bride which shall be made up from among those in the grave and those living.

Certainly the chariot that has come so suddenly upon the bride, in a moment, in the twinkling of an eye, is the same as that of Elijah and Elisha's day.   It was the chariot that belonged to the people of the Prince.

Soon, so very soon, the day will break across the darkness of this world, and the shadows will flee away at His coming!

CHRIST IS COMING! WE ARE WAITING

'Mid the shadows dim;
Longing till the night's dark pinions
Fold their plumes to Him.
Waiting for each gate of sorrow,
Thinking of the glad tomorrow;
Standing 'neath His banner, keeping
Watch while all the world is sleeping.
Christ is coming! Come, Lord Come!
Christ is coming! in a moment
Shall the shout resound,
And the voice of heaven's archangel,
And God's trumpet sound;
Then the sleeping saints arisen,
Bursting from their earthly prison,
With the living upward soaring,
See their Lord with eyes adoring.
Christ is coming! Come, Lord, come!

Heyman Wreford

vs. 13.   "RETURN, RETURN, O SHULAMITE: RETURN, RETURN, THAT WE MAY LOOK UPON THEE. WHAT WILL YE SEE IN THE SHULAMITE? AS IT WERE THE COMPANY OF TWO ARMIES."

She is gone; the bride has left in the chariot of the people of the Prince.

The cry of the daughters of Jerusalem, of those left behind goes out, "Return, return, return, return." Four times they beg of her to return. They long to see her just once more.

When the saints of God are raptured out of this world, this will be the cry of many many millions of souls. But it will be too late then.

"Be ye also ready, for in the hour that ye think not, the Son of Man Cometh!"

A little of the terror and confusion that will come upon the people when the blood washed, waiting saints are taken out of the way is revealed in Thess. 2:8, "Then shall that wicked be revealed."

It is only the presence of the saints who are the salt of the earth that is keeping this world from utter destruction right now.

"WHAT WILL YE SEE IN THE SHULAMITE? AS IT WERE THE COMPANY OF TWO ARMIES."

Some versions substitute "two armies" for "Mahanaim." What was Mahanaim? It was a town on the east of Jordon. The name signifies "Two hosts, or Two camps". It was given this name by Jacob in Gen. 32:1, 2. It was at this place that the camp of Jacob met with the camp of heaven, the hosts of angels.

I feel that the King James Version in its translation is very correct.

Just what will we see in the Shulamite, the bride of the King?

We will see, just what it says — as it were, the company of two armies, two hosts, two camps.

How then, can the bride which is one — as we see in 6:9, also be two?

She is one group made up of two armies. The army of the Saints that have marched out of the Old Testament and the army that are marching out of the Age of Grace.

Some may not believe that the Old Testament saints will be included in the bride of Christ. But why shouldn't they?

Elijah was a type of those who came out of grace—the chariot accompanied him.

Elisha was a type of those who came through death — the chariot accompanied him also.

When Esther, who was the queen, and type of the bride, won the great victory, who was it that had been her counsellor? Mordecai. Who was it that shared in her glory and reward? Mordecai. Esther had the house of Haman, but Mordecai was next to King Ahasuerus, great among the Jews, and accepted of the multitude of his brethren, seeking the wealth of his people, and speaking peace to all his seed. Esther 10:3.

Mordecai trained and brought up Esther. He is a type of the Old Testament saints which have been our teachers and example. 1 Cor. 10:11, "Now all these things happened unto them for ensamples: and they are written for our admonition, upon whom the ends of the world are come."

Heb. 11:40, 12:1, "God having provided some better thing for us, that they without us should not be made perfect. Wherefore, seeing we also are compassed about with so great a crowd of witnesses (the Old Testament Saints) let us lay aside every weight, and the sin which doth so easily beset us, and let us run with patience the race that is set before us."

Even as Esther came to the kingdom for "such a time as this", we have come also at this last hour, the end of the world, and all the Old Testament Saints are watching us. Are we going to fail? Are we going to come through victorious? They can not be made perfect without our assistance.

Mordecai watched Esther closely to see if she would make the conquest. His life depended upon her.

Let us remember the eyes of Abraham, Isaac, Jacob, Elijah, Elisha, Samuel, David, Isaiah, Jeremiah, and hosts of others are upon you and me.

CHAPTER SEVEN

vs. 1. "HOW BEAUTIFUL ARE THY FEET WITH SHOES, O PRINCE'S DAUGHTER! THE JOINTS OF THY THIGHS ARE LIKE JEWELS, THE WORK OF THE HANDS OF A CUNNING WORKMAN."

"HOW BEAUTIFUL ARE THY FEET WITH SHOES, O PRINCE'S DAUGHTER."

In chapter 4:1-5 we had a description of the bride, but it was incomplete. We only saw, as it were, the bust of the sculpture. For some strange reason, the writer at that time did not complete the picture. Now, we have the complete picture, beginning from the lower limbs, the feet, and coming slowly upward.

We must remember, that this is not the description of any living woman, but of the bride of Christ, the saints of God.

The Margin of the Revised Version gives the translation "How beautiful are thy steps."

What is it about the steps, or the feet of the Bride of Christ that brings rejoicing to the heart of the Bridegroom?

One of the last commands of the Lord Jesus before He left the disciples and the believers was, "Go ye into all the world and preach the gospel to every creature." Mark 16:15.

Now, the time of harvest is over; the bride has come home. The Lord is looking upon her steps. He sees the feet of the bride, shod in the sandals of Eph. 6:15. "Shod with the preparation of the gospel of peace." Her feet were always, at all times, prepared and willing to go forth with the gospel of peace to all places.

He says, "My child, your steps in my calling have been beautiful."

We are the daughters of The Prince. As we walk in royal dignity, we bring honour to God by our steps. If we fail, as so oft we do, and walk in the counsel of the ungodly, we bring dishonour and shame to the Royal Heavenly Prince, whose name we bear.

Isaiah, in ch. 52:7 under the anointing of the Holy Spirit, saw the great company of anointed men and women going forth in the last days preaching His word. "How beautiful upon the mountains are the feet of him that bringeth good tidings, that publisheth peace; that bringeth good tidings of good, that publisheth SALVATION; that saith unto Zion, Thy God Reigneth!"

"THE JOINTS OF THY THIGHS ARE LIKE JEWELS, THE WORK OF THE HANDS OF A CUNNING WORK-MAN."

In the first part we noticed the change in the translation from feet to steps. In the same way the word "joints" has been translated "turnings" or "windings."

This is very much in keeping with the context of the passage.

The turnings and windings of mountain roads are well known to travellers. It is almost necessary to go up a mountain by gradual degrees. The higher the mountain is; the more turnings and windings there are. Some hair-pin turns are so sudden that they are almost sickening. But the Lord says to the bride, "The winding and turnings that your feet have made have been the work of My hands."

Yes, the "Cunning Workman" is God. He is the One who has ordered our steps. Psa. 119:133.

We must say with the psalmist, "My feet were almost gone; my steps had well nigh slipped." Psa. 73:2.

But He has compassed us in our steps; by His grace alone we will continue climbing mountains and will not decline. Psa. 17:11 and Psalm 44:18.

Job, in the hour of his calamity, said, "Doth not He see my ways and count all my steps?" Yes, He does see our ways; He does count our steps. Job 31:4.

There may be times when we know not which way to take, but if in all our ways we acknowledge Him, He shall direct our paths.   Proverbs 3:6.

When we first arrived in Shanghai in 1947, we wanted immediately to go inland. The Lord kept us at the coast for 3 months. It was hard waiting, but later we knew why He had ordered our steps to stay, for at the end of three months the place, where we were going, fell to the Communists. God had been wise to delay us.

But the waiting was hard, and one of the comforting things was a little tract, a poem, sent me by a girl in Niagara Falls. Little did Shirley know how much it would mean to me. I have it with me now as I write and want to quote from it. In all our miles and years of travel, I have had this poem with me.

Part of it is —

> One step at a time simply trusting
> The One who is holding thy hand,
> The One who with infinite wisdom,
> Each step of thy pathway has planned.
> The Shepherd has marked out the pathway,
> The end from beginning He knows;
> But light He will give "As thou goest" —
> One step at a time Jesus shows.

vs. 2. "THY NAVEL IS LIKE A ROUND GOBLET, WHICH WANTETH NOT LIQUOR: THY BELLY IS LIKE A HEAP OF WHEAT SET ABOUT WITH LILIES."

"THY NAVEL IS LIKE A ROUND GOBLET. WHICH WANTETH NOT LIQUOR."

The Revised Version renders, "liquor" mixed wines. The original Heb. simply says "mixture".

In the study of midwifery, one of the most important things, and yet very simple, in the care of the newborn is the tying of the umbilicus cord. If it is not done tightly enough, the infant can easily bleed. It is easily understood that any blood, even an ounce, is of great value to the new born infant.

In Ezekial 16:4 we read of the birth of the Israelite nation. The Lord says that He found them unwanted and uncared for, and He came and took over their care as a doctor would that of a new born infant. He goes on to describe how the nation grew and became a strong and beautiful people but later were lifted in pride, and their hearts went after other gods.

The birth of the early church was cared for by the Lord in the same way. He took over the frightened, unloved, persecuted few, and they have become a strong and beautiful people.

You will notice that it says in this verse that there was no lack of liquor, mixed wine.

The beginning of the church did not lack in the power of God. From its birth it was indued with power from on High.

It is as though the Lord is saying that He took that new-born infant, the early church, and with the loving care of The Great Physician He tied that umbilicus cord perfectly, even as He did for Israel.

"THY BELLY IS LIKE AN HEAP OF WHEAT SET ABOUT WITH LILIES."

A great deal is said in the scriptures about the belly. The American Version has used the word waist. But whichever word is used it refers to the inner man, the depths of his being.

Of the wicked we read that in his belly he prepareth deceit. Job. 15:35.

The belly of the wicked shall want — be empty of good things. Prov. 13:25.

Of the saint of God we read — Out of his belly shall flow rivers of living water. John 7:38.

The inner life of the Christian is hid from the world quite often, but is revealed to the Lord. His word is a discerner of the thoughts and intents of the heart. Heb. 4:12.

The bride will not have hidden evil in her innermost being. She will be clean and pure like the lilies.

Wheat is a type of the word of God. Luke 8:11. The innermost being of the bride is like a heap of wheat. The bride is filled with the word of God.

In Job. 15:2 we read, "Should a wise man utter vain knowledge and fill his belly with the east wind?"

Vain knowledge when compared with spiritual knowledge is likened unto a belly full of wind.

The knowledge which comes by the revelation of the Word of God is the only thing that will profit a man's soul.

Jesus said, "It shall not be taken away." Luke 10:42.

vs. 3. "THY TWO BREASTS ARE LIKE TWO YOUNG ROES THAT ARE TWINS."

Once again the perfection of her love is mentioned, note 4:5.

vs. 4. "THY NECK IS AS A TOWER OF IVORY; THINE EYES LIKE THE FISHPOOLS IN HESHBON, BY THE GATE OF BATHRABBIM: THY NOSE IS AS THE TOWER OF LEBANON WHICH LOOKETH TOWARD DAMASCUS."

"THY NECK IS AS A TOWER OF IVORY."

In 4:4 we noticed that it described her neck as a tower of David.

Towers are fortified posts that are situated in exposed and dangerous places.

In the old days men soon discovered that those on higher places had the advantage over those below.

The bride of Christ lives on a higher plane than those around her. We need not be defeated all the time. We need not lose any battles at all. We have the advantage over our enemy.

Men of ancient times also found that their signals traveled farther when given from high places. So they built higher places in the walls of their cities, and they called these towers.

Yes, when we live in the higher spiritual realm we have better, immediate contact at all times with our allied forces. As we see Satan's hordes attacking our soul, we can immediately send out the cry for help, and the Lord will hear us because we are living close to Him.

So then, the Christian is rightly described as having his neck likened to a tower, for he walks with his head in the clouds, but his feet on the ground. Some times we hear it said that such and such a person has their head in the clouds. It is not so funny perhaps as it sounds. If we truly want to live close to God, we cannot grovel in the filth of this earth.

Why does it say ivory? That is the substance that was used by kings or wealthy men only in those days. The bride bears in her body the mark of royalty both in her neck, and also in her hair, as we will later see.

When people became free from the rule of feudal lords, they built belfry towers in the town squares. These towers were symbols of their new freedom.

"If the son therefore shall make you free, ye shall be free indeed." John 8:36.

By this description we are then also reminded of our freedom in Christ, freedom from earth's fetters.

"THINE EYES LIKE THE FISHPOOLS IN HESHBON."

Heshbon means "stronghold." It was the capital city of the Amorites. Num. 21:26. It stood on the western border of the high plain. Twenty miles east of Jordon, its ruins still mark its site. Even today, there are many cisterns among the ruins which bear witness of the fishpools that were throughout the city in Solomon's day.

Sihon, the Amorite king of Heshbon, refused to let the children of Israel pass through, and when he came against them in battle, God gave Israel the victory, and they defeated him and possessed his land which was one of very great power. Num. 21:21-25. This land was later divided among the tribes of Gad, Reuben, and the half tribe of Manasseh. Deut. 29:7, 8.

We have often seen fishpools in our parks. The water runs in fresh every day as the stale water runs out. It must be kept clean. Standing over the pool, we have looked down and watched the gold and silvery movements of these beautiful creatures God has made.

Eyes speak of spiritual insight. The word here is telling us simply, that the spiritual insight of the bride of Christ is as clear as the fishpools of Heshbon. She is able to see clearly and distinctly the movements and workings of God. There is no uncleaness or filth to hinder her from spiritually seeing God's revelation to her.

May God give us, each one who longs for it, the same spiritual insight into His workings and His wonders. May we reflect it from ourselves so that others will see God in us, as the passer-by sees the fishes of the fishpools.

"BY THE GATE OF BATH-RABBIM."

Bath-rabbim means "daughter of many". It was one of the gates of the city of Heshbon.

Perhaps this gate is mentioned because the fishpools could have been near it.

Travellers coming to the great stronghold of Heshbon upon entering through this gate would immediately be confronted with the beauty of these fishpools.

"THY NOSE IS AS THE TOWER OF LEBANON WHICH LOOKETH TOWARD DAMASCUS."

This is the third tower mentioned in this song.

The tower of Lebanon, it is believed, is the one which David built near Damascus, as mentioned in 11 Sam. 8:6.

Damascus from the time of Abraham has been one of the most important cities of the Syrians. According to Josephus, it was founded by Uz, grandson of Shem. David won a great victory over them and slew 22000 soldiers in battle. He ruled over it for a short time.

It was a city which later in the time of Solomon became an adversary to Israel. 1 Kings 11:24, 25.

In Solomon's time it gave him much trouble. His soldiers had to be constantly on guard. The place where they stood on guard against their adversary who had control of Damascus, was no doubt the tower of Lebanon near the city. Day and night they stood on guard with their faces looking toward that enemy's stronghold, keeping vigilance against the foe.

Even so, the Lord says that the nose of his child is as the tower of Lebanon, facing toward the place of danger, never ceasing to be on guard.

vs. 5. "THINE HEAD UPON THEE IS LIKE CARMEL, AND THE HAIR OF THINE HEAD LIKE PURPLE; THE KING IS HELD IN THE GALLERIES."

"THINE HEAD UPON THEE IS LIKE CARMEL."

Carmel means "fruitful place". It is one of the most striking mountains of Palestine. Its cliff rises 600 feet above the Mediterranean sea.

It was made famous by Elijah when God sent the supernatural fire from heaven.

With its foot in the waves and its head towering in the sky, it is a picture of the Bride of Christ who lives among the nations of the world, but whose head is lifted high above the sins of this world.

"THE HAIR OF THINE HEAD LIKE PURPLE."

The hair speaks of power as we mentioned before. She possesses the royal power of heaven. Purple is the colour of royalty.

The power we possess is not our own. He has given it to us.

"But we have this treasure in earthen vessels, that the excellency of the power may be of God, and not of us." 11 Cor. 4:7.

"THE KING IS HELD IN THE GALLERIES."

The American Revised reads, "The king is held captive in the tresses thereof."

As we mentioned before, hair speaks of power. The royal power, which we have received from God through our Lord Jesus Christ, is power not only in our dealings with man, but also power with God.

The King of Kings is held captive by the power of the bride. She holds a strange and fascinating power over her Bridegroom.

This is the authority that we have in Him, that "If ye ask anything in My name, I will do it. "John 14:14.

Remember Mordecai's great reward from the King. He and Esther were given the king's ring. This ring had the king's seal. Any order that was sealed with this seal could not be reversed. All the force of the empire stood behind it to bring it to pass. Ahasuerus, the king, told Mordecai and Esther that they could write for the Jews, "As it liketh you."

We have this same authority with God. He has given us His Name as the seal of the King of Kings. Whatsoever we ask in His name, as it pleaseth us, for the salvation of His people and the extention of His kingdom, we know that when we use His Name we have the armies of heaven behind us.

"I will hasten My word to perform it." Jer. 1:12.

vs. 6. "HOW FAIR AND HOW PLEASANT ART THOU, O LOVE, FOR DELIGHTS."

David knew the secret of how to delight and give great pleasure to the Lord. It was David's humble ways, his complete reliance upon the leadings of the Lord that won for him the delight and high pleasure of the Lord.

David said, in Psa. 18:19. "He delivered me, because He delighted in me." If we live to please the Lord He will deliver us from many afflictions and troubles.

If, however, on the other hand, we are deaf to the Lord's voice and blind to His leadings, and choose our own ways rather than the ways which would bring Him delight, then He promises the sword of judgment. Isa. 65:12.

If we hope to escape the great judgment that is coming upon the earth, we must learn now to obey His still small voice, to walk in His leadings, to do His will. Then, if we hear Him now, we will also hear the trumpet call that will deliver us from the hour of evil.

vs. 7.   "THIS THY STATURE IS LIKE TO A PALM TREE, AND THY BREASTS TO CLUSTERS OF GRAPES."

The palm tree. There are more than 1500 different kinds of palms. I am sure though, that the particular one which is referred to is the Royal Palm. Are we not children of the King. Then it is fitting that we should be likened unto the Royal Palm. The Royal Palm is one of the most beautiful of all the palm trees. Its great tall trunks resemble pillars that have been erected by a master architect.

We have heard and read about "Palm tree Christians". The Psalmist says that the righteous flourish like the palm tree. Ps. 92:12.

The palmyra palm of India has about 800 different uses. Not only is the tree beautiful then, but also it is the source of life to many people of tropical lands. If the palm tree was taken away from them, they would have to change their way of living.

The palm tree that produces fruit is known for its ability to produce its best fruit in old age.

The root of the palm tree is often the same length as that seen above the ground.

It will bend in the wind, but it is almost impossible to break off.

Putting all these things together, how beautiful then is this comparison of the Christian's stature being likened unto that of the upright palm.

Our lives are the sources of blessing to many.

As we walk with God, we need not fear old age and inactivity, for in our twilight years we shall be able to produce better fruit than in our youth.

The winds of affliction may bend us, but they will not break us.

Our roots are deep in the Love of God.

"AND THY BREASTS TO CLUSTERS OF GRAPES."

The love and affection of the bride of Christ is likened unto clusters of grapes.

The cluster of grapes which the spies brought back to the children of Israel was so large that two men had to carry it between them. Num. 13:23.

The Christian whose love is perfect could be likened unto these perfect and almost miraculously oversized grapes.

When the children of Israel were rebellious, the Lord likened them unto wild grapes. Grapes when they are wild and uncared for become small and sour. I remember having wild grapes on our farm in Ontario which were impossible to eat.

The fruit that the vine produces is a revelation of how it has been cultivated, pruned and cared for.

The pruning must hurt, but it will encourage us to remember that it perfects our love for Him.

vs. 8. "I SAID, I WILL GO UP TO THE PALM TREE, I WILL TAKE HOLD OF THE BOUGHS THERE-OF: NOW ALSO THY BREASTS SHALL BE AS CLUSTERS OF THE VINE, AND THE SMELL OF THY NOSE LIKE APPLES;"

"I SAID, I WILL GO UP TO THE PALM TREE, I WILL TAKE HOLD OF THE BOUGH THEREOF:"

The branches (boughs) of some palm trees have leaves that may grow 3 or 4 feet broad and 10-20 feet long. The raffia palm has huge feather-like leaves that commonly become 50 feet long and 8 feet wide.

The branches of the palm were used by the Jews as tokens of victory and peace.

In Rev. 7:9 we read of the great multitude which no man could number, of all nations, and kindreds and people, and tongues, standing before the throne, and before the Lamb, clothed with white robes and having palms in their hands, crying, "Salvation to our God which sitteth upon the throne and to the Lamb."

So we see that the branches also are a token of praise to God.

The Lord says that He dwelleth in the praises of His people. No wonder then, that if we produce perfect boughs, we shall bring glory to the Lord by victory, peace and praise. He will surely take hold of the boughs thereof.

The American revised version says, "I will climb up into the palm tree, I will take hold of the branches thereof." Yes, he will come and dwell in the midst of our sacrifices of praise. Some Christians produce small withered boughs of praise. Some produce average boughs of praise. Others are like the raffia palm with it's great boughs and these minister to the Lord in a continual anointed spirit of praise to Him.

"AND THE SMELL OF THY NOSE LIKE APPLES."

The American Revised has translated it, "The smell of thy breath."

Bad breath often reveals sickness and corruption within. Perhaps also it might be a sign of tooth decay.

Spiritually speaking we should be pure and healthy Christians and breathe out, like our Lord did, the Fullness of God's Spirit from within us.

If we are filled with corruption we will breath out corrupttion.

The breath of the smoker is tainted with his filthy habit.

The breath of the drinker of strong drink is sour and vile.

The breath of a baby is sweet and pure.

The Lord breathed upon His disciples after He was risen from the grave, and they were endued with the power of the resurrected Lord. He said to them, "Receive ye the Holy Ghost:" John 20:22.

If we have the fullness of Christ in us, and His Holy Spirit dwelleth within, then, we also should breath forth the sweetness and fragrance which the Lord expects of us, His bride.

> "Breath on me, Breath of God",
> Fill me with life anew
> That I may love what Thou dost love,
> And do what Thou wouldst do.
>
> Breath on me, Breath of God,
> Until my heart is pure,
> Until with Thee I will one will,
> To do or to endure.
>
> Breath on me, Breath of God,
> Until I am wholly Thine,
> Till all this earthly part of me
> Glows with Thy fire divine.
>
> *Edwin Hatch, 1885.*

vs. 9. "AND THE ROOF OF THY MOUTH LIKE THE BEST WINE FOR MY BELOVED, THAT GOETH DOWN SWEETLY, CAUSING THE LIPS OF THOSE THAT ARE ASLEEP TO SPEAK."

The American Revised Version has divided this verse in two parts. The first part signifying that they are the words of the Bridegroom and the second are the words of this bride. Looking at it in this way, let us take it in its parts.

"AND THY MOUTH LIKE THE BEST WINE."

Several times the speech of the bride has been mentioned in this book. Her speech has been likened to the honeycomb and milk, 4:11. Also the words of redemption typified by the thread of scarlet and the comeliness of her speech is mentioned in 4:3. The sweetness of the voice of the bride is mentioned in 2:14.

In 5:1 we read that the bridegroom has accepted and received the gifts of honeycomb, milk and wine.

When the disciples were filled with the Holy Spirit, such a transformation took place in their speech that the on-lookers thought they were filled with new wine.

Peter standing up with the eleven said, "Ye men of Judea and all ye that dwell at Jerusalem, be this known unto you, and hearken to my words: For these are not drunken, as ye suppose, but this is that which was spoken by the prophet Joel, in the last days, saith God, I will pour out My Spirit upon all flesh: and your sons and your daughters shall prophecy, and your young men shall see visions, and your old men shall dream dreams; And on my servants and on my handmaidens I will pour out in those days of my Spirit, and they shall prophecy." Acts. 2:14-17.

The Holy Spirit, of whom wine is a type, is the source of this anointed speech. Whether it be prophecy or praise or the anointed tongues and interpretations, or any of the oral gifts of the Holy Spirit, all these precious gifts can only come forth from a mouth that has been anointed by the power of the Holy Spirit.

The Bride of Christ in the last days, is going to have a greater anointing upon her than ever before. She will fulfil the prophecy of Joel 2:28, 29.

It says again in this verse in Song of Songs. "And thy mouth like the best wine."

When the Lord turned the water into wine it was at the end of the feast. The guests said, "Thou hast kept the best wine for the last."

Yes, the Lord gave good wine at the beginning of the feast of Pentecost, when the early church was started in the outpouring of the Holy Spirit, but He has again kept the best for the last.

When Jesus provided the wine in Cana, it was the first of His known miracles and the revelation of His power. So again, when the best of wine is in the mouth of His bride, it will be a revelation to the world that Jesus is the Messiah.

"THAT GOETH DOWN SWEETLY, CAUSING THE LIPS OF THOSE THAT ARE ASLEEP TO SPEAK."

Or, "that goeth down smoothly" as in the American Revised. The Heb. word is "Aright".

How fitting! It is the right of every saint of God to be filled with this best wine. There is a plenteous supply. No one needs to go without. He said, "Come, buy wine and milk, without money, and without price."

As to the supply, we are told that the fats shall overflow with wine and oil. Joel 2:24.

"Fats" is the old English word for vats. Vats are large vessels or cisterns, and are able to hold a great quantity of liquid.

It is for us; this wine is for each child of God. Not only is it for the preachers, teachers and evangelists but for every layman.

When the early church needed seven men as laymen to wait on the tables, they said, "Look ye out seven men, filled with the Holy Ghost and wisdom." Why should waiters need to be filled with the Holy Spirit?

This is to show us that we all can be and we all should be filled with His Holy Spirit. "For the promise is unto you, and to your children, and to all that are afar off, even as many as the Lord our God shall call." Acts. 2:39.

Yes, the promise is for the waiter in the restaurant, the fireman as he fights the fire, the sailor on the seas, the coolie on the street, the maid in the kitchen, the boy on the ball park, the girl as she does household chores, the teacher in the school room, the beggar on the street, who will no more be a beggar after that. It is for all, this wonderful promise.

It is our "right", our "inheritance" our "gift from the Lord." Have you received your portion?

"CAUSING THE LIPS OF THOSE THAT ARE ASLEEP TO SPEAK."

What is the advantage of this precious gift? What does it do for the Christian?

It tells us in this verse. Lips that are asleep will suddenly be touched with the coals from off the altar and be awakened to speak forth the oracles of God.

Many Christians have no power to witness because their lips are sleeping; they have not tasted the wine, which gives quickening and enduement of power for service.

When I was a Christian only a short while, I called to my father in the other room, "Daddy, I have been saved a month today." A few days later a young man, a Roman Catholic, who had heard me say that to dad, asked me a strange question. He said, "Were you nearly drowned this summer or what happened to you?" I asked him what he meant, and he told me how he had heard me tell my father I had been saved a month, and he wondered what I meant by that.

Oh how I longed to tell him, but I just was not able. I couldn't say a single thing about the Lord; I weakly answered, "No, I wasn't nearly drowned; I meant something else."

The subject was closed, but oh, how badly I felt, — Like a weakling, ashamed of the Lord.

Several days later, in the same week, I was wonderfully filled with the Holy Spirit in my bedroom while praying with my mother and a girl friend.

That evening I waited for this young man to come home from work, and while he was eating his supper, along with a friend of his, I came into the dining room and said, "Bill, you wanted to know what I meant by being saved. I couldn't tell you when you asked me, but I can now." And with the precious anointing of the Holy Spirit upon me, I, a babe in Christ, began to speak the words of salvation, giving scriptures and explanations on the Word as I had never done in my life. It wasn't I; it was He. But what a difference was made in my life from the hour I drank of His "better wine."

Truly, the lips that have been asleep to the revelations from His word will be awakened to speak forth the deeper truths, when they have drunk of this heavenly wine.

vs. 10. "I AM MY BELOVED'S AND HIS DESIRE IS TOWARD ME."

Wonderful Jesus! His only desire, His only love is us. He has no other interest. We are His one desire. To win us to Himself and present us before the throne of His Father in obedience to the will of God is His greatest desire.

So many lovers and so many families are broken up, because one of them is not sure of the other's love. Often a spirit of jealousy will possess one when he is not sure of the love of the other.

Not so, is our relationship with the Lover of our Soul. We need never doubt His love for us. His desire is toward me; toward each one of us personally.

vs. 11. "COME, MY BELOVED, LET US GO FORTH INTO THE FIELD; LET US LODGE IN THE VILLAGES."

The anointed bride, who has been drinking of the wine of the Holy Spirit, is now ready for service. She wants to go out into the fields, into the villages; she wants to labour for Him, and with Him.

She calls Him to go with her. She knows that if she goes alone, that her ministry will be a failure.

Moses knew how fruitless was the effort of man when he goes forth without the presence of God. He had tried once before in his own strength to deliver the people, but had only brought confusion, rejection, and years of wasted time.

Now Moses wants to be sure of God in all things, and in all leadings, and he says, "If thy presence go not with me, carry us not up hence." And then he adds, "For wherein shall it be known here that I and Thy people have found grace in Thy sight? Is it not in that thou goest with us?"

The presence of Jesus with us is a sign to the world that we have found His grace.

Jesus promised us this wonderful blessing before He left us. He said He would be our Co-Worker. He said, "Go, ye into all the world and preach the gospel to every creature, and Lo, I am with you alway, even unto the end of the world. Amen." Matt. 28:20, Mark 16:15.

As he was with Peter, John and Paul, He will be with us. But we must call, as the bride does, "Come, my Beloved, Let Us go."

vs. 12. "LET US GET UP EARLY TO THE VINEYARDS; LET US SEE IF THE VINE FLOURISH, WHETHER THE TENDER GRAPE APPEAR, AND THE POMEGRANATES BUD FORTH: THERE WILL I GIVE THEE MY LOVES."

In 6:11 the bride goes down herself, alone, in self-examination and heart-searching. Now she calls Him to come with her.

She wants to be perfect in His eyes. So often we cannot see our own mistakes and sins; we need Him to point them out to us, to reveal them to us.

"LET US SEE IF THE VINE FLOURISH, WHETHER THE TENDER GRAPE APPEAR," Together with Him, who is all tenderness and love, she searches her heart to see if her love is, as He said it was, a cluster of grapes.

Let us see if the love of the bride of Christ is flourishing. This is the call of the Christian. The Lord said that in the last days, the love of many shall wax cold. Matt. 24:12. He said it would be because iniquity would abound.

The Christian who is careful to keep sin out of his heart, will not find his heart waxing cold easily.

"AND THE TENDER POMEGRANATES BUD FORTH:"

These two are the important things in the life of the saints of God.

1. His love for the Lord and others.
2. His righeous acts.

The pomegrantes, as we said before, 6:11 and 4:3 speak of Holiness and Righteousness. The soul who has these two qualities — love and holiness, is perfect before God.

"THERE WILL I GIVE THEE MY LOVES."

The A.R.V. has put it, "love".

I think it just means that all her affection, — all the love that is in her heart will be poured upon the Lord as they rise early to work together.

What better way to show our Lord our love, than to labour for Him, to be willing to burn out for Him.

Every deed we do is an offering of our love for Him.

Every moment spent alone with Him, even though away from others, is a token of our love for Him. It shows how truly we prefer Him before all others.

vs. 13. "THE MANDRAKES GIVE A SMELL, AND AT OUR GATES ARE ALL MANNER OF PLEASANT FRUITS, NEW AND OLD, WHICH I HAVE LAID UP FOR THEE, O MY BELOVED."

"THE MANDRAKES GIVE A SMELL."

The Mandrake is mentioned twice in the Bible. It was known in early times for its strange contents which acted like a narcotic and anesthetic. The Arab's called it "Devil's apple", because of its ability to stimulate sensual desires. It was used in early times in making "love-potions." The plant grows like a lettuce. The roots are large and shaped like a carrot. The white flowers grow on its stalks. The fruit is about the size of a small apple, red or yellow. It has an agreeable odour and taste.

We could call it the fruit of love. The bride had it in the garden of her heart, such an abundance of this fruit of love that the fragrance of it was smelt in the air which her Beloved breathed as He walked with her.

"AT OUR GATES ARE ALL MANNER OF PLEASANT FRUITS, NEW AND OLD, WHICH I HAVE LAID UP FOR THEE, O MY BELOVED."

She has been preparing for His coming. The fruits are laid up, waiting for His arrival. They are all for Him. How busy she has been!

Both new and old, — the gifts of a life time. The ones she prepared in her youth, and those she prepared in old age. Some of the fruits are old; they were perhaps laid aside from the hour she first knew Him. Others are new; she has only just gathered the last ones for Him.

"I have laid up for thee, O my Beloved." Yes, she did it all for Him.

There may have been times when she wondered if He cared, wondered if He would come to see her labour of love. Some times we get discouraged, and think our work is vain, it is true. Yet now He is coming, and she tells Him how she has prepared for this hour, ever since she first loved Him.

"For God is not unrighteous to forget your work and labour of love, which ye have shewed toward His name, in that ye have ministered to the saints, and do minister." Heb. 6:10.

Don't give up, keep gathering in the fruits, ministering to the saints, working for Him, doing all things in His name, knowing that your labour is not in vain. "Therefore, my beloved brethren, be ye stedfast, unmoveable, always abounding in the work of the Lord, for as much as ye know that your labour is not in vain in the Lord." 1 Cor. 15:58.

How many have given up just when He was about to reward them for their efforts, and in so doing, have lost His note of praise, "Well done, thou good and faithful servant, enter thou into the joy of the Lord." Yes, if we are faithful over a few things, He will make us ruler over many things. Matt. 25:21.

From "God Calling" the following quotation —

"In a race it is not the start that hurts, not the even pace of the long stretch. It is when the goal is in sight that heart and nerves and courage and muscles are strained almost to breaking point.

So with you now the goal is in sight, you need your final cry to Me. Can you not see by the nerve and heart rack of the past few days that your race is nearly run. Courage, courage. Heed My voice of encouragement. Remember that I am by your side, spurring you on to victory.

In the annals of heaven, the saddest records are those that tell of the many who ran well, with brave stout hearts, until in sight of the goal, of victory, and then their courage failed. The whole host of heaven longed to cry out how near the end was, to implore the last spurt, but they fell out, never to know until the last day of revealing, how near they were to victory."

CHAPTER EIGHT

vs. 1. "O THAT THOU WERT AS MY BROTHER, THAT SUCKED THE BREASTS OF MY MOTHER! WHEN I SHOULD FIND THEE WITHOUT, I WOULD KISS THEE, YEA, I SHOULD NOT BE DESPISED."

"O THAT THOU WERT AS MY BROTHER, THAT SUCKED THE BREASTS OF MY MOTHER!"

The bride. is thinking how pleasant it would be if her Lover were not only her well Beloved, but also that there might be some tie by blood. In the times of the writing of this book, often a man had many wives. The different children of these wives sometimes fell in love with each other, as happened in the case of David's son, Amnon, when he fell in love with his half sister Tamar.

However, there were those who were born of the same mother and father, and that was the closest relation of the entire family. These would stick by each other in all circumstances and fight for one another, as we have seen by the way in which Absalom slew Amnon for the grief and shame he had brought on his sister. Absalom and Tamar both had the same mother Maachah, the Geshurite princess.

With all Absalom's faults, we must not forget his intense love for his sister and the grief he felt for her sorrow. When he had a daughter he called her Tamar also, probably in honour of his sister, whom he loved so dearly. 11 Sam. 14:27. She also was as beautiful as her father and her aunt, and was his only daughter. She had a daughter by the name of Maachah who married Rehoboam, and her husband loved her more than all of his 18 wives and 60 concubines. 11 Chron. 11:18-23. Her son became the next king, King Abijah of Judah.

Some of this is out of context with the thought of this verse, but it is just to make us realize the close relationship which existed between children of the same mother.

This intimacy, which the bride shows a desire for, is perhaps on she had never had in her own family. We remember that she had earlier expressed how her brothers and sisters had not held this loving attitude toward her, which she had longed for and seen in others.

The love which she reveals in her heart is a very refreshing and pure love. There is no taint of the impure sexual attractions which are labeled "love" today.

"WHEN I SHOULD FIND THEE WITHOUT, I WOULD KISS THEE: YEA, I SHOULD NOT BE DESPISED."

How spontaneous is her demonstration of love! In the entire song this perhaps reveals the love in her heart more than any other thing she has said.

We remember the sinful woman who came into the house of the Pharisee and expressed her love to the Lord by freely kissing his feet. Jesus said to the Pharisee, "Simon, thou gavest me no kiss."

There is the kiss of the betrayer, as Judas gave our Lord in the garden. It was the lowest thing any man could do. It compelled the Lord to speak in astonishment, — about the only reproof He uttered all through His hours of passion, "Betrayest thou, the Son of Man with a kiss? That which had before been the kiss of a friend, a brother, became the kiss of cruelty and betrayal. The Lord knew that a kiss was a sign of affection and reverence. How wrongly it was misused that night in the garden!

The kisses of the bride of Christ for her beloved are those of affection and reverence. I am sure that if we could see Him, we would wish to throw ourselves at his feet as Mary Magdalene did in the garden of the tomb and demonstrate our love and reverence to Him in the only way that we humans know.

God gave us this way of expressing our love. With some it may be only a ritual and have no meaning. At other times it is a sudden and voluntary display of spontaneous love, and that is when it is warming and comforting.

The kiss which the bride wishes to give is the kiss of welcome. She says, "When I should find thee without, I would kiss thee."

He would know how much His companionship was desired by the way in which He would be welcomed by His own.

He came unto His own, and they received Him not. They had no kisses for Him, only the cross. But through His love, He has won the kisses and love of heathens and Gentiles for 20 centuries from every tribe, tongue and nation, from the east and the west, from the north and the south. There are those who feel in their hearts that lovely pure affection for Him, which the bride so beautifully expresses for us all.

"YEA, I SHOULD NOT BE DESPISED."

The world looking on can not understand why we should love Jesus so. They think us odd. They despise us for that which to them seems unnatural.

How many have suffered because of their love for the Lord! Wives have persecuted husbands; husbands have persecuted wives; children have risen up in rebellion against their families, and parents against children. Many have had to live in the midst of fire, and others have given their lives for their love.

vs. 2. "I WOULD LEAD THEE, AND BRING THEE INTO MY MOTHER'S HOUSE, WHO WOULD INSTRUCT ME: I WOULD CAUSE THEE TO DRINK OF SPICED WINE OF THE JUICE OF MY POMEGRANATE."

"I WOULD LEAD THEE, AND BRING THEE INTO MY MOTHER'S HOUSE."

Once before in, 3:4, she says that she did bring Him into her mother's house. Again she expresses how welcome her life and home is to His presence.

We often see the motto, "Christ is the Head of This House." Her mother's home was the only one she had, but He was welcome there.

If the Lord were to have His rightful place in our Christian homes, what love and peace would rest upon the household! People would immediately sense the presence of the Christ as they walk in the door. The spirit of the people prevails over the whole household. If it is one of contention between husband and wife, it usually enters into the hearts of the children. Children are very susceptible to the emotions and attitudes of others. I have seen children take on the same feeling as the rest of the household in things which did not concern them and really didn't ordinarily interest them.

Let us bring the Lord into our homes. Let us be like little children, open to Him, impressionable to His sweet Spirit of tenderness, love and peace. If He is the head of our household, we will take on His Spirit and become susceptible to Him as our children are to us.

How we love the words of Joshua, "As for me and my house, we will serve the Lord." Joshua 24:15.

"WHO WOULD INSTRUCT ME."

The pronoun "who" has been added by the translaters. It makes it seem as though it is the mother who is the instructor. But I am sure it means the One whom she will lead into her home.

The Lord is truly our instructor. He is our teacher. In all our affairs, whether among men or in the intimacy of our homes, we need His daily instruction and guidance. This He has already promised us when He said, "I will instruct thee in the way which thou shalt go; I will guide thee with mine eye." Psalm 32:8. How gently He can teach and instruct us in all His ways if only we will be of a teachable and easily-lead spirit!

He admonishes us not to be as the horse or mule, which have no understanding: whose mouth must be held in with a bit and bridle. Ps. 32:9. Such people never can get very far in the lessons of their Instructor. They never leave primary school. But if we follow on to know the Lord, we shall be taught

— 151 —

of the Lord, and great shall be the peace of our children. Yes, the Lord, given His rightful place as the instructor of the lives of those in our homes, will bring peace upon the household.

"I WOULD CAUSE THEE TO DRINK OF SPICED WINE OF THE JUICE OF MY POMEGRANATE."

There in the home that is welcome to Him, He not only is the instructor, for He is treated as more than a teacher. He also is given the hospitality of the choicest of guests. Her very best wine which she has saved for years, comes out of the wine cellar in His honour and is freely offered to Him. The wine which has come from the fruits of her own labours, is from her own garden, not that which was purchased on the street, but her own.

How often we housewives, visiting our friend's house, will ask when tasting some delicious jam or pickle or such, "Did you make that?" And the friend so proudly answers "Yes, I did, but it didn't turn out very good." Although she knows that it seldom has tasted better, but she wants to give the impression that she is capable of making it even more delicious.

So, the bride says, she will give Him the wine from her own pomegranates.

I am sure that to Him the gift of her love meant more than if it had been a necessary purchase brought in at the last minute. It showed that she had been waiting for Him and had prepared earlier for His coming.

The pomegranate, as we remember, is a type of the righteous acts of the saints. And all those deeds which the Bride of Christ has done over the years of her Christian experience shall be poured out for Him as a gift of love.

vs. 3. "HIS LEFT HAND SHOULD BE UNDER MY HEAD, AND HIS RIGHT HAND S H O U L D EMBRACE ME."

As we have already studied some of these verses, we will refer to the orginal, found in 2:6.

vs. 4. "I CHARGE YOU, O DAUGHTERS OF JERUSALEM, THAT YE STIR NOT UP, NOR AWAKE MY LOVE, UNTIL HE PLEASE."

This is her final challenge that nothing should come between her and her Lord.

vs. 5. "WHO IS THIS THAT COMETH UP FROM THE WILDERNESS, LEANING UPON HER BELOVED? I RAISED THEE UP UNDER THE APPLE THREE: THERE THY MOTHER BROUGHT THEE FORTH: THERE SHE BROUGHT THEE FORTH THAT BARE THEE."

Yes, the bride is coming up out of the wilderness experiences in a more intimate relationship with her Beloved Lord than she ever had before. She is coming up out of years of dryness, years of testing, years of backslidings and murmurings into the inheritance which is hers through Him, upon Whose arm she leaneth.

Let us link our arm through that of our blessed Lord; let us not fear; we are going forth with the Conqueror to conquer.

In these last days, the cry of the Spirit is going out over the church, "Arise and shine: for thy light is come, and the glory of the Lord is risen upon thee. For Behold, darkness shall cover the earth, and gross darkness the people: but the Lord shall arise upon thee, and His glory shall be seen UPON thee." Isa. 60:1, 2.

Yes, glory to the Lord, His glory will be seen upon His bride, not any glory of her own, but His glorious, eternal, everlasting anointed glory. It will be seen upon those who are coming out of the wilderness leaning upon their Beloved.

"I RAISED THEE UP UNDER THE APPLE TREE: WHERE THY MOTHER BROUGHT THEE FORTH;"

How well we remember the day we were saved, and with what tenderness the Lord received us unto Himself, forgiving us and washing us clean in His precious blood!

In the same continued tenderness He has raised us up, daily, constantly caring for us as a Father careth for His children.

In 2:3 the bride said she sat herself down under the shade of this apple tree. She said His fruit was sweet to her taste.

Yes, He is the apple tree. We were born again under the gentle wooing of the Holy Spirit. Just why He should save us we cannot understand. Why, from amongst the millions and millions who are lost and in sin, He should set His love upon us, we will never understand. But He has, and it humbles us and fills us with gratitude and praise.

Still, through life, He remains the apple tree, under whose shadow we find comfort and rest. From the fruit of His branches He feeds us and cares for us. We lack nothing; we possess all things; with great delight we grow up in Him, under the shadow of His branches.

vs. 6. "SET ME AS A SEAL UPON THINE HEART, AS A SEAL UPON THINE ARM: FOR LOVE IS STRONG AS DEATH; JEALOUSLY IS CRUEL AS THE GRAVE: THE COALS OF FIRE, WHICH HATH A MOST VEHEMENT FLAME."

"SET ME AS A SEAL UPON THINE HEART."

The seal mentioned here is the signet-ring. In Heb. it is "chotham." Sometimes it was worn around the neck by a chain and therefore would be near the heart. It was one of the most important possessions that a man had. If he should lose his signet or seal, and it would fall in the hands of a wicked man, it would be the same as if someone could perfectly forge our signature today. The possessor of the seal had authority.

The prayer of the bride is that He whom she loves might stamp her image upon His heart so that she would have first place in His affections. It was as though she wanted Him to write her name upon His heart as a sign to all the world that she belonged to Him.

Not only that, but she knew what authority the seal carried, and if she was given this privelege, she would have unlimited authority with the heart of her Beloved.

Has He done that, Has the Lord set us as a seal upon His heart? In 11 Tim. 2:19, we read, "Having this seal, the Lord knoweth them that are His." Yes, He knows, and He will never forget, for we are sealed until the day of redemption upon His heart.

"AS A SEAL UPON THINE ARM."

This, no doubt, refers to the signet-ring which was worn upon the hand as in Esther 8:8.

Perhaps the bride did not even realize what she was asking. of her Lord when she said these words. But He heard her prayer, He saw her longing, and He has given her that which she asked of Him.

In Isa. 40:16. He calls to her, "Behold, I have graven thee upon the palms of My hands:"

He cannot use His hands, but what He is reminded of His bride.

The seal was made with two long spikes. It was made by the hands of cruel and wicked men. It was made for those cruel and wicked men.

The day on Calvary's hill, when Jesus Christ stretched open His hands to allow the nails to be driven through His flesh, I am sure, He must have thought of the words of Song of Solomon, as the bride said to Him, whom she so dearly loves, "Set me as a seal upon Thine arm." And again He no doubt recalled His promise and prophecy to her which had gone out through the prophet Isaiah some 250 years later. "Behold I have graven thee upon the palms of my hands."

The Hands of our Lord, bearing the seal of the nail prints, speak out that we who trust in Him belong to Him.

"FOR LOVE IS STRONG AS DEATH."

Who can fight death? When the angel of death walks into the sick room, all the doctors in the world and all medical aids cannot fight it.

Only the power of the resurrected Lord can defeat and has already defeated death.

So it is with love; it is strong; it walks into the heart and never ever can be conquered by man. It puts its roots into your heart and only leaves when the heart stops beating in death.

When someone has killed the love in another person's heart, perhaps part of the heart has died with it. Certainly it leaves its mark upon the personality and the spirit of the man.

Many say they have loved, who have not loved at all.

The Love the bride is speaking about is the love that is as as strong as death. It was love that led to death.

The love of God which compelled Him to lay down His life for us. "Hereby perceive we the love of God, because He laid down His life for us: and we ought to lay down our lives for the brethren." 1 John 3:16.

"JEALOUSY IS CRUEL AS THE GRAVE."

How cruel and hard it seems to the loved one, to lay that dear one away in the bowels of the black earth and let it remain there until it turns to dust.

On a cold winter night the wife thinks of her husband lying there under a blanket of snow while the icy winds blow over the grave. How much nicer it would seem if they could, upon death, simply be carried away body and soul into the presence of the Lord by His holy angels! Yet for this we must wait until the resurrection morn.

Jealousy is cruel; it is hard. It is like the grave. Even as the body of the loved one cannot by his own strength fight against the mound which lies upon him, and rise up again, so the soul that is possessed by a spirit of jealousy is helpless against it in his own strength.

Yet, God can deliver a man and woman of this spirit of ungodly jealousy.

Jealousy is often aroused by suspicions of unfaithfulness in love and rivalry of affections.

The bride of Christ need never fear or have any jealous feelings towards her Beloved. He has upon His heart her image, and upon His hands the seal of His love. He wears these as a sign of His promises of betrothal even as she wears those which He has given her, as we mentioned in 1:10.

"THE COALS THEREOF ARE COALS OF FIRE, WHICH HATH A MOST VEHEMENT FLAME."

No, we need never be jealous of Him, but oft by our waywardness and lack of love for Him, we have made Him jealous over us.

He has confessed His jealousy to us, He says, "For I the Lord thy God am a jealous God."   Exodus 20:5.

The jealousy which the bride sees as a fire is none other than the jealousy of God Himself.

This is not an evil spirit of jealousy from the devil. The devil has his counterpart in this even as he has in all the things of God.

This is the Holy Jealousy of a Holy God, the Righteous Jealousy of a Righteous God.

It is jealousy that is aroused by the rivalry of the devil for the affections and souls of His bride.

It is the same jealousy that Paul felt in his heart for the Corinthian church when he said "For I am jealous over you with godly jealousy: for I have espoused you to one Husband, that I may present you as a chaste virgin to Christ."   11 Cor. 11:2.

The question is asked in 1 Cor. 10:22, "Do we provoke the Lord to jealousy?" Ask your heart that question. What loves rival for the affections of your heart?

Yes, the bride caught a picture of the jealousy of God when she said that it was a most vehement flame, for remember, "Our God is a consuming fire." Deut. 4:24.

vs. 7. "MANY WATERS CANNOT QUENCH LOVE, NEITHER CAN THE FLOODS DROWN IT: IF A MAN WOULD GIVE ALL THE SUBSTANCE OF HIS HOUSE FOR LOVE, IT WOULD UTTERLY BE CONTEMNED."

"MANY WATERS CANNOT QUENCH LOVE, NEITHER CAN THE FLOODS DROWN IT:"

Both Jonah and the Psalmist said, "All Thy waves and Thy billows are gone over me." But the Psalmist, likely a Levite who was detained in Northern Palestine and who longed to be back in the temple worshipping and serving God added another beautiful verse. "YET, the Lord will command His loving-kindness in the daytime, and in the night His song shall be with me, and my prayer unto the God of my life."

Yes, he knew that though many waters of affliction had gone over him, still the Lord loved Him, and his own love for the Lord was strong enough to stand the test. Psalm 42:7, 8.

In the verse just before this, the bride said that jealousy was as the most vehement flame.

Most fires can be quenched with water, but the flame of love which the bride is speaking about is so powerful that all the waters of affliction poured upon it, still cannot quench this love which she has for her Lord.

Jeremiah loved God like that. When the waters of persecution were poured upon him, he said, "I will not make mention of Him, not speak any more in His name. But His word was in mine heart as a burning fire shut up in my bones, and I was weary with forbearing, and I could not stay." Jer. 20:9.

What is this fire that was poured out upon the followers of Jesus Christ in the upper room? It was certainly more than power and zeal; I believe it was also the flame of a greater love for the Lord.

Before I was saved, I remember a song that was popular at that time. Some of the words were, "I don't want to set the world on fire, I just want to start a flame in your heart." That is what the Lord wants to do in our hearts. He wants to start a flame in our hearts that will burn in us like the burning bush, an everlasting flame that will never go out. When God makes a flame, it is an everlasting one. However, the Lord wants to do more than set a flame in our hearts; He wants to set the world on fire with the flame that is in our hearts.

Nothing will help you to work for God more than the flame of love. Let us ask Him to set our hearts aflame with His wonderful love.

The flame of God's love is as that of an oil well on fire. If you pour water on it, it would turn into a greater fire than before. So when we have the true love of God in our hearts, the waters of affliction and persecution will only spread it and make it a greater flame.

All who have lived in China have heard of the terrible day when Chungking, a city on the Yangtze river was set on fire. The fire began in the godowns, I have heard, and spread more and more. People from the other side of the river came across on small boats to see the fire. But the sparks flew out and ignited the oil tankers that were in the harbour of the river. These exploded, and soon the river was a river of fire, and thousands died on the river as they were trapped in the flames. It was a sight of horror and terror.

Even as the fire of God's love cannot be quenched by water, so the fire of God's anger and judgment cannot be quenched, but it is an everlasting fire. Matt. 18:8.

"IF A MAN WOULD GIVE ALL THE SUBSTANCE OF HIS HOUSE FOR LOVE, IT WOULD UTTERLY BE CONTEMNED."

The value of love can never be estimated. It is priceless.

The man who said these words was one of the wealthiest kings that ever lived. Solomon lived in the midst of the greatest splendour that ever was given any Israelite, man or king. As he looked around his home, probably about 160,000 square feet of royal palace, what did he see? - - - :

Four rows of the cedar pillars of Lebanon supported the great state hall which was open on special occasions.

Next, the important porch of judgment was supported by columns. This hall of judgment stood opposite the first great state hall.

The third building, called a porch of pillars, was the ordinary place of business, the room in which the king received ordinary visitors and in which he transacted the business of the kingdom usually.

The fourth was the inner court, having gardens, and fountains and surrounded by cloisters (covered walks).

The fifth was the courts of the women and harem.

The sixth was the court of the attendants and guards.

The seventh was the palace of Pharaoh's daughter who was too proud and important a person to be grouped with the ladies of the harem.

In fact all the wealth of the country went into the splendour of his palace, the temple and the building up of Jerusalem and purchases of horses, etc.

Yes, Solomon could have looked around at all this as he said, "If a man give all the substance of his house for love, it would be utterly scorned."

We may be poor in earthly substance, but if we have the love of God, we are more than millionaires. I would rather be a pauper loved by God than a prince upon whose head the wrath of God resteth.

> The love of God, is greater far,
> Then tongue or pen can ever tell
> It goes beyond the highest star,
> And reaches to the lowest hell.
> The guilty pair, bowed down with care
> He gave His son to win,
> His erring child, He reconciled
> And pardoned from His sin.
>
> Could we with ink the ocean fill
> And were the skies of parchment made,
> Were every stalk on earth a quill
> And every man a scribe by trade.
> To write the Love of God above,
> Would drain the ocean dry
> Nor could the scroll, contain the whole,
> Though stretched from sky to sky.

vs. 8. "WE HAVE A LITTLE SISTER, AND SHE HATH NO BREASTS: WHAT SHALL WE DO FOR OUR SISTER IN THE DAY WHEN SHE SHALL BE SPOKEN FOR?"

As we have mentioned before, the breast speaks of affection and love.

The bride who is prepared and ready for the place she is to fulfil in the plan of God is rightly concerned for those whom she loves who are not of marriageable love.

Her sister is younger, her sister is not matured in the things of God.

What a picture this poor little sister is, of many Christians today! She should be ready, for the hour is coming soon when she will be spoken for. Her name will be called. The marriage supper of the Lamb, is almost here, and our brothers and sisters in the Lord are not ready; their love is not yet made perfect.

Oh, brother and sister, it is time that we awaken our hearts to concern for those who are our own brothers and sisters in the Lord.

The Bible not only tells us to pray for the sinner, but also it tells us many times to pray for one another, to pray for the saints, etc.

My own heart often asks the question as I see a brother and sister who seems so immature in Christ, "Are they ready, if Jesus should come today?"

The Bride is talking to the Bridegroom about her sister. Let us talk to the Lord about our brothers and sisters, let's plead for them with Him that they might be perfected in the Love of God and be ready for the hour when they will be spoken for.

vs. 9. "IF SHE BE A WALL, WE WILL BUILD UPON HER A PALACE OF SILVER: AND IF SHE BE A DOOR, WE WILL INCLOSE HER WITH BOARDS OF CEDAR."

"IF SHE BE A WALL, WE WILL BUILD UPON HER A PALACE OF SILVER:"

The Margin of the revised has given the word "battlement" for palace.

One of the most wonderful promises in the word of God to His children is the one, "They shall fight against thee, but they shall not prevail against thee: for I am with thee to save thee and to deliver thee, saith the Lord" Jer. 15:20.

But most of us don't know the first part of this great promise even though we know the later part so well, and that is, "I will make thee unto this people a fenced, brazen wall."

If we will throw ourselves upon the Lord He will make us into walls that are firm and brazen. Walls that will not crumple when the earth quakes, the typhoons and tornados sweep through the land and when the enemy drops the atomic bomb, our walls will still stand firm.

What is this wall? In Amos 7:7 we read of a wall made by a plumbline. Yes, and the Lord stood on this wall with another plumbline in His hand. He said to Amos, "Amos, what seest thou?" "Behold, I will set a plumbline in the midst of my people Israel: I will not again pass by them any more."

The plumbline is used by the builder, and the Lord is the Master builder of the wall. Today He is standing upon the wall of the Old Testament saints and He is measuring us. How do we, as the bride of Christ fit into the wall? The plumbline will soon indicate if there is any projection in the wall, for the wall must be absolutely vertical.

Only living stones can go into the wall of salvation. Any thing that is substituted for the blood of Christ will reveal itself. "For the stone shall cry out of the wall, and the beam out of the timber shall witness against it." Habakkuk 2:11, 12, "Woe unto him that buildeth a town with blood, and stablisheth a city by iniquity."

"In that day shall this song be sung in the land of Judah: We have a strong city; salvation will God appoint for walls and bulwarks." Isa. 26:1.

The Lord has said that our walls are continually before Him. Not for one moment will He forget the wall which He has built from our lives. We are precious in His sight. Isa. 49:16.

Isa. 60:18, "Thou shalt call thy walls SALVATION, and thy gates PRAISE."

How wonderful, what a heritage is possible for this little sister! The Lord promises His bride, if she be a wall of salvation, He will, with the help of His bride, build beautiful towers of silver upon her wall. Silver is a type of redemption. How glorious she will be when He completes His work in her! Can't you just picture the shining towering battlements resplendent in the noon day sunshine.

"IF SHE BE A DOOR, WE WILL INCLOSE HER WITH BOARDS OF CEDAR."

What is the door? According to Isa. 60:18, it is her life of praise. The highest thing that she can attain to is that she might be a door of praise unto the Lord.

"Open Ye the gates, that the righteous nation which keepeth the truth may enter in. Thou wilt keep Him in perfect peace whose mind is stayed on Thee." Isa. 26:2, 3.

When the gates of praise are open and God's people become a people of praise, not only will peace abide within the gates, but many shall come in.

The Lord wants us to praise Him not only with our lips, but also with our lives. But an offering of praise from an unclean vessel is a mockery in the face of God.

The boards of cedar speak of the eternal life, which will surround those who are doors of praise.

Enclosed forever with the cedar speaks of that which is eternal, that which will not allow corruption to pass through. We are ever safe in His love, surrounded by His eternal care for us.

vs. 10. "I AM A WALL, AND MY BREASTS LIKE TOWERS: THEN WAS I IN HIS EYES AS ONE THAT FOUND FAVOUR."

The original Hebrew gives the word, "peace" instead of "favour." Although "favour" gives a nice thought, still it is perhaps not the full meaning like the word "peace."

What is the bride saying? She knows her position in the Lord. She knows that she is a wall. She knows that He has perfected that which concerneth her. Her love for the Master Builder is as a mighty tower upon the wall.

Her Beloved looking upon her knows full well that she has found her peace in Him. We link this up with Isa. 26:1-4, that beautiful song which the bride will sing, and we find that the secret of her walls of salvation which stand eternally secure against the foe, is the peace in which she abides by keeping her thoughts and imaginations stayed upon Him, with her full trust and confidence in Him alone at all times.

Is there trouble within our wall? It could be because we allow our minds to be troubled and our imaginations to be stirred until our trust in the Lord is shaken. Then our praise will stop, the gates will close, and our walls will begin to decay. The watchmen of the walls will become indifferent. Then they will begin to persecute the bride, and our city will be open to the attacks of the Evil one. We will become a city besieged by the enemy.

vs. 11.   "SOLOMON HAD A VINEYARD AT BAAL-HAMON; HE LET OUT THE VINEYARD UNTO KEEPERS; EVERY ONE FOR THE FRUIT THEREOF WAS TO BRING A THOUSAND PIECES OF SILVER."

"SOLOMON HAD A VINEYARD AT BAALHAMON; HE LET OUT THE VINEYARD UNTO KEEPERS;"

Baal-Hamon means "Lord of a multitude."

It could be the same place as the town mentioned in Joshua 19:28, as Hammon.

Solomon had many vineyards, Ecc. 2:4. This one, it is believed, was much vaster than any of the others. As he was too busy to care for these vineyards, he would put them in the charge of keepers.

"EVERY ONE FOR THE FRUIT THEREOF WAS TO BRING A THOUSAND PIECES OF SILVER."

This vineyard apparently must have been very fertile and profit-making. The keepers willingly gave 1000 shekels for its produce. This is about $335.00 U.S.C. In return for that, they were allowed to eat all the fruit they wanted, sell what they could, and have a profit of 200 shekels.

In Isa. 7:23 we read of the profitable vineyards which were reckoned at a silver a vine. "A thousand vines at a thousand silverlings."

vs. 12. "MY VINEYARD, WHICH IS MINE, IS BEFORE ME: THOU, O SOLOMON MUST H A V E A THOUSAND, AND THOSE THAT KEEP THE FRUIT THEREOF TWO HUNDRED."

The bride has her very own vineyard of which she is in charge. She will give unto the Lord that which is His share and unto the keepers that which is their portion.

How much does that leave for her? Only the fruit. But the true bride of Christ is content with just that much.

We are not here to make profit for ourselves. The vineyard which is the world, is put in our care. If we are faithful stewards of it we will hear his, "Well done."

All the silver goes to Him. It rightly belongs to Him. It was purchased by His precious blood.

The bride of Christ has charge of the vineyard in the absence of the King of Kings. She cares for it and gathers in the fruit. Surely she is permitted to eat all the fruit that she cares to eat. 1 Cor. 9:7. But she must be careful in her business transactions. She must sell her produce at a profit so that He can have His share.

Under the law, the children of Israel were the keepers of His vineyard. What did they do? They killed the Owner's Son, the Saviour of the world. They gave no silver to the Owner because they were full of greed and seized for themselves that which rightly belonged to Him alone. So the Lord told them what would be their punishment. "He shall come and destroy these husbandmen, and shall give the vineyard to others." Luke 20:16.

That is what He has done. He has taken it from the unworthy, wicked keepers and put it into the hands of other keepers. But are we doing much better? Have not the Gentiles persecuted and killed many who were the Lord's servants?

But the true bride who is faithful to the Lord will give unto Him, that which is His. She will seek nothing whatsoever for herself. Her joy is not in the profit, but in the service.

How many today love filthy lucre more than justice! They do not give the Lord His portion of that which He has intrusted into their care. These have no part in the true bride. The bride has no thought for herself. She says, "Thou must have a thousand." Let the keepers who have worked under her have the 200. She wants only to have His fellowship with her in the garden.

vs. 13.   "THOU THAT DWELLEST IN THE GARDENS, THE COMPANIONS HEARKEN TO THY VOICE: CAUSE ME TO HEAR IT."

"THOU THAT DWELLEST IN THE GARDENS."

Even as the Lord came down into the garden of Eden and walked with Adam and Eve, He today dwells in the garden, which is the place of communion with Him.

How is the place cared for? Is it oft neglected? Have the weeds grown around the prayer bench?

"Prayer is of many kinds, but of whatever kind, prayer is the linking up of the soul and mind and heart to God."

"So that if it is only a glance of faith, a look or word of Love, or confidence, and no supplication is expressed, it yet follows that supply and all necessary are secured."

"Because the soul, being linked to God, united to Him, receives in and through Him all things. And the soul, when in human form, needs, too, the things belonging to its habitation."

Taken from "God Calling."   May 31.

"THE COMPANIONS H E A R K E N TO THY VOICE: CAUSE ME TO HEAR IT."

The companions are those who accompany the bridegroom in His wedding. They are those who are with the Lord in glory, who are seated around His throne.

Perhaps they are the angels, and they may also be the saints of the Old Testament. But we know this, that they live in the realm where they constantly hear the voice of her Beloved.

She longs to hear Him too. She cannot in herself. But if she is willing, He will open her ears to hear His voice.

The place in which she will find the desire of her heart is the garden of communion.

> I come to the garden alone
> While the dew is still on the roses
> And the voice I hear, falling on my ear,
> His love to me discloses.
>
> Oh! He walks with me and He talks with me,
> And He tells me, I am His own,
> And the joy we share, as we tarry there,
> None other, has ever known.

vs. 14. "MAKE HASTE MY BELOVED, AND BE THOU LIKE TO ROE OR A YOUNG HART UPON THE MOUNTAINS OF SPICES."

The song closes with the yearning cry of the bride for the return of the Lord.

This is much like verse 17 in chapter 2. In that cry she mentioned the mountains of Bether, which means "division." There was a great division then between her and her Beloved. That was the division of time, but now the time is finished, and no more does she speak about those mountains which hindered His coming.

Now the separation is forever removed, and He comes to her from the mountains of spices.

You may remember that He told her in 4:6 "Until the day break, and the shadows flee away, I will get me to the mountain of myrrh, and to the hill of frankinsense."

He has been waiting for "daybreak". And now it has come, and the bride is standing on tip-toes waiting for His return. She is calling Him to make haste to her, to flee away from the place of His tarrying and receive her unto Himself, that where He is, she may be also.

> Oh, how I long for that city,
> My home with the angels above
> Safe in the vale with my Saviour,
> Sharing His wonderful love.
>
> Toils of the road will seem nothing,
> All shadows will vanish away;
> Heartaches and burdens all over
> Hasten, O glorious day!
>
> When will you come, Lord Jesus?
> When will you come for me?
> Oh, how we love Thy blessing,
> But sweeter Thy face to see.
>
> *P. C. Spiers*